INSTRUCTOR'S MANUAL

to accompany

Gurak/Lannon

STRATEGIES FOR TECHNICAL COMMUNICATION IN THE WORKPLACE

Lee Scholder, J.D.
University of Minnesota

Longman

Upper Saddle River   San Francisco   New York   Indianapolis   Columbus   Boston
Toronto   Montreal   Paris   Munich   Milan   Madrid   London   Dubai   Cape Town   Amsterdam
Tokyo   Taipei   Singapore   Seoul   Hong Kong   Sydney   Sao Paulo   Mexico City   Delhi

Instructor's Manual to accompany Gurak/Lannon, *Strategies for Technical Communication in the Workplace*

Copyright ©2010 Pearson Education, Inc.

1 2 3 4 5 6 7 8 9 10–OPM–12 11 10 09

Longman is an
imprint of

www.pearsonhighered.com

ISBN 10: 0-205-69906-5
ISBN 13: 978-0-205-69906-3

CONTENTS

Instructor Resource Center

Getting Registered

To register for the Instructor Resource Center, go to www.pearsonhighered.com and click **"Educators."**

1. Click **"Download teaching resources for your text"** in the blue welcome box.
2. Request access to download digital supplements by clicking the **"Request Access"** link.

Follow the provided instructions. Once you have been verified as a valid Pearson instructor, an instructor code will be emailed to you. Please use this code to set up your Pearson login name and password. After you have set up your username and password, proceed to the directions below.

Downloading Resources

1. Go to http://www.pearsonhighered.com/educator and use the "Search our catalog" option to find your text. You may search by Author, Title, or ISBN.

----

2. **Select your text** from the provided results.

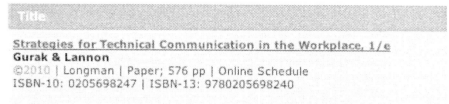

Strategies for Technical Communication in the Workplace, 1/e
Gurak & Lannon
©2010 | Longman | Paper; 576 pp | Online Schedule
ISBN-10: 0205698247 | ISBN-13: 9780205698240

Part of series: MyTechCommLab Series   MyTechCommLab Series

3. After being directed to the catalog page for your text, click the **Instructor Resources** link located under the **Resources** tab.

Clicking the Instructor Resources link will provide a list of all of the book-specific print and digital resources for your text below the main title. Items available for download will have a ⬛ icon.

----

4. Click on the View Downloadable Files link next to the resource you want to download.

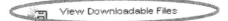

A pop-up box will appear showing which files you have selected to download. Once you select the files, you will be prompted to login with an Instructor Resource Center login.

----

5. Enter your login name and password, and click the **"Submit"** button.

----

6. Read the terms and conditions and then click the **"I accept"** button to begin the download process.

    I accept (proceed with download)

    Cancel (closes this window)

----

7. **"Save"** the supplement file to a folder you can easily find again.

Once you are signed into the IRC, you may continue to download additional resources from our online catalog.

Please "Sign Out" when you are finished.

vi

CHAPTER I

Introduction

This instructor's manual contains information, tips, exercises, and quizzes to help you effectively use *Strategies for Technical Communication in the Workplace* in your classroom.

The manual begins with a chapter providing you with overall teaching strategies for you to consider as you develop and implement your course. The chapter includes an overview of key features and tips for working with the publisher's Web site, MyTechCommLab™, which has a plethora of resources for you and your students to engage with material addressing technical and workplace writing. In addition, you will find a couple sample syllabi for your consideration.

Each of the successive chapters is numbered according to the chapter numbers in the book. Each contains a summary of the textbook chapter, teaching tips for that chapter's topic, additional exercises, and a 12-question quiz consisting of true-false, multiple-choice, and short answer questions. Answers to these quizzes can be found in the Chapter Quiz Answers section at the end of the manual.

Teaching this type of communication course can be extremely rewarding for students and instructors alike. Because this type of course requires real-world contexts and applications, as an instructor, you will learn much about the different fields your students work or want to be working in. Your students will find themselves stretching beyond the patterns they have become familiar with in academic writing, developing new ways of viewing communication that involve informed choices based upon the audience and purpose of each of their communications. Together, you and your students will emerge from your course experience with a shifted perspective. We hope you enjoy the journey!

1

CHAPTER II

Overall Teaching Strategies

This chapter provides you with some helpful approaches for teaching technical communication.

- Keeping rhetorical analysis at the forefront
- Pacing and project planning in your course
- Integrating group work into your assignments
- Working with the "Let's Get Started" exercises
- Leveraging the appendices in the text
- Using the MyTechCommLab™ Web site
- Creating a course plan: two sample syllabi

KEEPING RHETORICAL ANALYSIS AT THE FOREFRONT

One of the most exciting aspects of teaching technical communication courses is its direct application to real-world, applied contexts that have meaning for your students. Students write for specific readers in specific situations with specific goals in mind. For most of your students, this will be a very different way of thinking about writing. To provide support for your students in realizing they need to make adjustments for the audience, purpose, and context of the communication, you might try the following strategies:

- Ask students to specify the audience, purpose and relevant context considerations for *each* document they submit. As encouraged in the text, you might have them submit a completed Audience and Use Profile (in Chapter 4) with most, if not all, of your assignments.

- In peer reviewed assignments, ask students to take on the role of the audience the writer specifies.

- Use a variety of examples from the real world (provided by you and students) of each type of document to discuss in class—ask what audience considerations drove or should have driven the decisions made for each document.

PACING AND PROJECT PLANNING IN YOUR COURSE

Most technical writing courses will include one long project for students to complete—either a formal analytical report or a formal proposal. As the sample syllabi in this manual model, it is helpful to have several assignments build on each other so that students can work progressively toward the final project assignment rather than having to cram all of the pieces together at the end of the course. This extended process to complete an assignment is an important lesson in project planning. Students need to know that they will need time for clarifying their topic, completing both primary and secondary research, analyzing their findings, drafting and designing their report, getting feedback, and revising.

Have students select their individual topics early in the semester and then have several of the assignments refer specifically to this project of their choice. Frequent points of feedback from you and peers can help students stay on track as well as make important adjustments along the way. Potential assignments to help with pacing might be the following:
- Memo to instructor proposing topic
- Proposal that includes a full statement of purpose, audience, and research plan, including the overall research questions and what research strategies might help answer those questions
- Draft of surveys and/or research questions for peer review and instructor feedback
- One or two progress reports
- Final report draft
- Oral presentation of problem, research process, findings, analysis, and recommendations
- Revised final report

INTEGRATING GROUP WORK INTO YOUR ASSIGNMENTS

As you design the assignments for the course, include at least one team project that runs across several weeks, allowing for the team process to unfold. Admittedly, any collaborative project can have disappointing results for instructors and students alike. But even a project that proves disastrous can go a long way toward teaching students something about accountability and shared responsibility.

In designing group projects, you might consider a number of strategies:

- <u>Schedule in-class time for some group work:</u> It can be very helpful to allow some in-class time for a limited amount of this teamwork, partly so that you can observe the team dynamics and encourage questions in a face-to-face format. But, it's also extremely valuable for students to have experience collaborating both in the face-to-face context and through distance technology.

- <u>Set up Web-based collaborative spaces for groups:</u> You can help students work in an asynchronous mode by setting up online collaborative spaces for students to work in such as a designated discussion area in a course management system, a wiki, or a blog (see Chapter 18 for more information on wikis and blogs).

  Many course-management tools also include synchronous modes such as live chat rooms that could add another dimension to the remote group-work experience. As an alternative, you might have students explore their own online collaborative tools to use instead, but this might lead to students questioning you on a wide range of technologies. What you want to be careful of is having the students getting confused by the tools they are using, stifling the group work they need to do. Therefore, limiting the options to a few tools you as an instructor are familiar with, may help you be knowledgeable enough to guide students if they need extra coaching.

- <u>Ask students to share, at the beginning of their team process what their project plan will be.</u> The Project Planning Form is a great tool for groups to use early on and submit to you for accountability.

- <u>At the completion of a team project, include an opportunity for individual reflections on the team process.</u> This allows them to more fully integrate the lessons learned from the experience. Since plans almost always change, you might also ask students to reflect on what changed compared to their original plan. You could also ask them to

5

discuss what kind of group conflicts may have occurred along the way, the potential source of those conflicts, and how the group handled them. Finally, they might also share what lessons they might carry forward into their team projects in the workplace.

SPEAKING EARLY AND OFTEN

Though the oral presentation chapter is the last in the chapter, the concept of oral presentations should not be last in your instructional design. Throughout the course, your students should be engaging with each other through short, frequent oral communications, either as individuals or as groups during in-class exercises. This will help them become more comfortable with their peers as an audience and will make any final assignment you may have in oral presentations much less intimidating.

WORKING WITH THE "LET'S GET STARTED" EXERCISES

Beginning in Chapter 8, each chapter begins with a "Let's Get Started" exercise. By having students complete this exercise right away, even before you have covered the chapter, you help prime students for the key issues they will be learning. Provide a limited period of time to complete this exercise, perhaps a 15 to 20 minute in-class writing exercise before you cover this chapter. It might even be helpful to do this at the end of class the week before you cover the chapter.

Reassure students that if they don't know how to approach the task initially, that is OK, since they will be using the letter writing exercise as a self-check at the end of your time addressing the chapter's material. To avoid having students trying to make their piece "perfect" from the start, and to encourage them to actually complete the exercise, you might hold these in a sealed envelope at the beginning of the week. Once you have covered the chapter contents, you can re-distribute their initial versions to evaluate once they have worked with the chapter contents. The "Let's Get Started: Review" application at the end of the chapter guides students in a group exercise for this evaluation.

LEVERAGING THE APPENDICES IN THE TEXT

A key skill for students to walk away with is the ability to be a self-directed writer who makes use of resources to further sharpen their abilities. To this end, make frequent use of the appendices in the text as you progress through your course as reference sources for specific issues. While most areas of technical communication do not have one right or wrong answer, there are certain aspects that are, indeed, that clear: documentation of sources (addressed in Appendix A) and grammar/punctuation/mechanics/usage issues (addressed in Appendix B). **For these types of issues, avoid the temptation to edit your students' work for them!** Instead, refer them to key resources in the appendices so that they can find their own answers and correct their own work. You can simply specify the issue and point the student to the area in the appendix. You might consider using some of the shorthand descriptions suggested at the beginning of Appendix B.

USING THE MYTECHCOMMLAB™ WEB SITE

A well-written textbook is an excellent resource for teachers and students alike. But even the best textbook cannot possibly present all of the material relevant to such a complex topic as technical communication. A book providing complete coverage would be so large it would need wheels. Therefore, Pearson Education has created MyTechCommLab™. This site offers further reading, illustrations, exercises, templates, and access to the most current information available.

The MyTechCommLab™ site includes a wide range of material covering technical communication issues that are useful to instructors and students using any technical communication textbook. This site is located at http://www.mytechcommlab.com/.

MyTechCommLab™ is intended to be a comprehensive resource for technical communication students and instructors, and there are ongoing efforts to add even more resources to the site. So, don't be surprised to find even more expanded resources than those summarized in the following pages. The site contains eight main categories, which we'll discuss in more detail below:

- Model Documents
- Writing Process
- Research Process
- Document Design and Graphics
- Grammar and Usage
- Instructor Resources
- Grade Tracker Basics

Model Documents

This section of MyTechCommLab™ covers a range of document genres and purposes such as letters, proposals, reports and research reports, memos, instructions and procedures, definitions and descriptions, emails, and more. There are several types of resources in the Model Documents section (found within the two subsections labeled Model Documents and Activities and Case Studies).

Model Documents. In this section, you will find static PDF files showing examples of each writing genre (memos, reports, instructions, etc.), interactive annotated documents, and quizzes related to each genre of writing.

When you reach a particular genre in your class, students could compare the different approaches to writing the type of document reflected in the PDF and annotated examples and consider the different rhetorical choices made by the writers. Often, students look at one example and view that as THE solution for all similar documents. Comparisons help students understand that there isn't a magic all-encompassing solution to technical writing problems, but rather careful selections based upon the audience, context, relationships, purpose, and genre conventions.

By viewing the interactive annotated documents as well as the static PDF documents, students become more engaged in the material and deepen their connection with it. Virtually all technical communication courses include assignments or exercises involving critiquing one or more existing documents for various components (audience, visual design, organization, writing style, etc.). Encourage students to review these interactive examples to model this type of critical thinking. Each of these interactive resources provides a rhetorical analysis of a particular document, noting how particular rhetorical tools are being used. Some of these interactive documents have the heading "Revision Challenge," in which case the commentary focuses on ways in which the document might have been written differently to be more effective.

The quizzes are short answer fill-ins that can help you gauge student understanding of the key purposes and conventions associated with the different genres. After students have learned about a particular writing genre, you can use these as quick in-class quizzes if you are in a computer lab, or as an at-home assignment for students to complete online. Unlike the multiple-choice quizzes

8

on other parts of the site, there is not automatic feedback for students on these quiz answers. Students submit these to you via the Grade Tracker, and you provide the feedback and grades.

Activities and Case Studies. Organized by document type, this section includes more than 65 different activities involving writing documents in response to specific scenarios or documents. In many of the exercises, students fill in a textbox with their document critiques, rewrites, or suggested initial versions of a document. For others, students are asked to revise the document Also provided are corrected versions or commentary on what should have been revised in the document for greater effectiveness. There are rich resources here for your assignments and in-class labs.

Near the end of this section is a series of case studies that address usability of specific genres of writing. These cases studies provide scenario-based technical communication problems for students to solve. They are generally more challenging, with more questions to consider and tasks to complete, than the Activities. As such, they may be particularly appropriate after students have had a chance to work with the Annotated Examples and Activities and after you have guided them through some in-class discussion. Since the concept of usability arises in various ways throughout the text, these case studies might be helpful to incorporate one at a time, at progressive stages of the course, as your students' knowledge of usability issues deepens over time. Results from the case studies can be submitted to you for grading via the Grade Tracker tool.

Writing Process

Writing Process: Tutorial. Through a series of brief exercises, this section leads students through various stages of the writing process by having them complete exercises and submit them for your review. You can focus on specific steps at critical points in the class projects to help students move along and for you to check their progress. You might also ask them to do a mini trial run of the entire writing process by completing one or more of the Guided Essays, which focus on different purposes for documents—to inform, analyze, evaluate, or recommend. The Guided Essays move students through all stages of the writing process in a step-by-step sequence by having them write at each stage of the process. Since this aspect of the tutorial moves linearly from one step to the next, rather than a more iterative process, students may find it very challenging for a project of any

9

length. If you help students focus on a very narrow, focused topic, they may find these Guided Exercises more useful.

Writing a Formal Report: Tutorial. Formal analytical reports are among the most common documents produced by technical communicators, and most technical communication courses include this as one of the main final deliverables. This tutorial focuses specifically on the skills and strategies students need to master, and the decisions they need to make, in creating a formal report. Unlike the Process Tutorial, which includes exercises requiring students to generate their own written thoughts for instructor feedback, the Formal Report tutorial is an instructional tool only, with explanations and examples woven throughout. This resource on the MyTechCommLab™ reiterates the overall structure noted for formal reports in Chapter 16 of *Strategies for Technical Communication in the Workplace*, including examples of front and end matter components.

Writing and Visuals. Given the central role of visual communication in technical writing, this is an excellent trove of resources for your students to explore. This section includes articles providing specific strategies for evaluating visual communication, multimedia resources that engage learners in explorations of specific documents, and exercises involving different scenarios that students can respond to and submit their answers to you for feedback via Grade Tracker.

Activities and Case Studies. This section refers back to the Activities and Case Studies also listed in the Model Documents section of the site and described earlier.

Web Links. This annotated list of valuable Web resources about writing includes links that take students to technical communication and to writing guides, grammar resources, sites with additional quizzes and exercises, usage and style guides, lists of common errors, ESL resources, and more. If you intend to send students to a list of links, it is helpful to have a clear purpose in mind. For example, in the early part of the course, where students are exploring the concept of technical communication as a professional field, you might have them explore the organization links and journals to and identify three topics in the field they find interesting.

Student Bookshelf. This section includes two PDF files listing texts you might consider using parts of to supplement the text's readings. The book *Academic Literacy* largely focuses on academic rather than work contexts, but the text does

10

include an interesting discussion of Rhetorical Tools for Academic Writers that could easily be applied in the technical writing context. The second book, *Workplace Literacy*, is obviously much more on point. You might find the last chapter particularly helpful when discussing the technical communication field. The use of the phrase "professional communication" here may seem much more accessible to some students, and the summaries of benefits of being a professional writer and the skills needed are seeds that may motivate your students to take on the learning required to be effective.

Research Process

It's easy to become overwhelmed by the amount of information available to us in this information-laden culture we have created. MyTechCommLab™ includes a number of resources to help students find ways of locating relevant, credible sources, and determine how to synthesize this information and integrate it into their final documents.

MySearchLab™. MyTechCommLab™ links to Pearson's proprietary research site, MySearchLab.com, which offers detailed step-by-step guidance through the research process, online research tools, and access to four robust business and academic databases such as EBSCO and Link Library. This is a great place to start when you begin covering Chapter 3 in the Gurak and Lannon text, and again as your students pursue their more extensive project assignments which may require in-depth research. MySearchLab also includes other resources to help students in their writing and research process, including an auto citation tool for MLA, APA, and CBA style as well as a brief introduction to how to avoid plagiarism through proper attribution of resources.

The Research Assignment. While this section largely focuses on academic writing assignments rather than the more applied business-oriented writing projects your students will work on in your course, the materials on finding sources and integrating sources are helpful addendums to *Strategies for Technical Communication* and the other materials on the MyTechCommLab™ site. Many of these resources are multimedia, with audio and visual components to help engage your students more fully in the material.

Avoiding Plagiarism. Are you looking for a one-stop site to give your students a thorough view of how to use sources responsibly? This resource is a gem. Split into two sections for MLA and APA style documentation, the site includes

11

detailed examples with practice exercises with detailed automated feedback (the student responses are also tracked with Grade Tracker), and an extended analysis section where students review a longer section of a document and specify which documentation problem is applicable (automated feedback coaches them to the right answers here).

Student Bookshelf. This area is linked from all of the main sections of the MyTechCommLab™ site. This section provides supplementary texts you might consider adding to your course readings. They are helpful for providing alternate perspectives or more in-depth attention to specific topics. Related to research, the bookshelf includes Branscomb and Barrs' text *Research Navigator Guide to English*. Your students may find many of the strategies related to finding and working with secondary resources helpful.

Document Design

The whole issue of visual design of documents may at first seem foreign to students who may be accustomed to writing only in the academic setting. Your role is largely to sensitize them to the visual elements of message design and to help your students learn the criteria for making wise choices about how and when to integrate different visual strategies.

Visual Rhetoric Tutorial. The five main sections of this tutorial—Elements of Visual Rhetoric, Using Visuals, Types of Visuals, Color, Document Design— will help your learners understand how to make strategic decisions in this area. Each of these sections includes a number of prompts for both group discussion and writing exercises. This would be an excellent tutorial for students to complete early in the course to gain an overview of the main principles of visual design.

Web Design Tutorial. This tutorial focuses on teaching students the basics of setting up a Web page, concentrating primarily on HTML coding. The text's emphasis, by contrast, is on the design features and usability issues of Web design, no mention of the more technical aspects of HTML coding. Nevertheless, you might find this tutorial a useful supplement to the text if you want to expose your students to the back-end view of Web pages. In a world of WYSIWYG tools, one might wonder how much HTML knowledge is necessary for someone not charged with developing high-end Web sites. Nevertheless, even when using template-driven Web generation tools or blogging tools, it can be helpful to know how to tweak the visual design with slight changes to the HTML.

Web Links. This section includes an annotated list of valuable Web resources for document design and graphics, including design guides, outlines for effective design, tools to help in thinking visually, and guidelines for how to skillfully include images, graphs, tables, or photographs into documents.

Student Bookshelf. This area is linked from all of the main sections of the MyTechCommLab™ site. Related to visual design, the Bookshelf includes Susan Hilligoss's supplement, *Visual Communication*, Second Edition, for learning how to analyze design decisions and how these decisions contribute to the overall effectiveness of a written piece.

Grammar and Usage

For a variety of reasons, students may enter your class without the basic skills needed to write clearly and effectively. Many students may have been schooled during a period in our education when there was less of an emphasis on the basic mechanics in favor of a more freestyle, expressive writing approach. Grammar, punctuation, mechanics, and judicious sentence style were not necessarily emphasized or valued. In our increasingly diverse college environments, we also find many students who have come to English as a second language. MyTechCommLab™ provides several resources to help build students' skills in these key tools of technical writing.

Diagnostics. By having students complete one of the diagnostic tests at the beginning of your course, you can help students identify key areas they need to concentrate on in order to strengthen their writing skills. The site includes two comprehensive 50-question diagnostics to evaluate your students' current command of skills in sentence grammar, basic grammar, punctuation and mechanics, and sentence style. Their results page will identify overall strengths and weaknesses, as well as provide specific question-by-question feedback and allows them to email their results to you.

ExerciseZone. This section of the site includes thousands of practice items organized into 10-question practice sets on over 50 topics. Topics include Sentence Grammar, Basic Grammar, Punctuation and Mechanics, Usage and Style, Sentence Editing, and Paragraph Editing. Results pages provide question-by-question feedback and provide options to read more about the topic in an

13

online handbook or practice more with other practice sets. Results can also be emailed to the instructor.

ESL ExerciseZone. Designed specifically for your ESL students, this section of the site includes almost 700 exercises, organized into 10-question practice sets, targeted at areas most troublesome for speakers of multiple languages. To keep your students from becoming overwhelmed with so many options, focus their attention on the most pressing issues in their writing. Once they have mastered those, move to the next issues.

Longman Online Handbook. This concise handbook provides explanations for the grammar points tested in ExerciseZone, as well as brief Check Yourself activities. Students can use it to read about topics either before or after they measure their skills in ExerciseZone.

Web Links. This annotated list of valuable Web resources about grammar and writing provides URLs that lead to writing guides, grammar resources, sites with additional quizzes and exercises, usage and style guides, lists of common errors, ESL resources, and more.

Instructor Resources

This area of the site includes several resources to help you in both using the site and in running your class.

- How-to manuals on using the Grade Tracker tool in MyTechCommLab™
- Pearson Technical Support Information
- A link to the Instructor Resource Center, where you will find a wide variety of digital resources to support you as an instructor
- Information about a subscription-based plagiarism analysis tools that allow you to submit student papers for analysis.

Grade Tracker Basics

When you are signed in as an instructor, you will have access to the Grade Tracker tool. As you can see from our descriptions of the various resources, the site is full of exercises and activities that students can submit. You can view student responses for the various attempts made and provide feedback and grades for essay questions. This is a great alternative to the paper shuffle of in-class exercises or the nightmare of having to track a ton of emails and email attachments from your students.

CREATING A COURSE PLAN: TWO SAMPLE SYLLABI

Below, you will find two versions of the scheduling portions of a course syllabus. You will see a version for a 15-week course and one for an 11-week course. The main difference is that the in-class user testing of the instructions is dropped and the materials on employment correspondence are dropped from the shorter course. Since students generally have access to career center workshops and resources, the employment materials are one area that is often dropped from communications courses. You will want to encourage your students to avail themselves of existing campus resources, regardless of whether or not you cover employment documents in your class. Another difference for the quarter version, you will see one less week for oral presentations, with slightly shorter versions of this assignment.

In addition to these elements, most syllabi include the following key elements— your university will likely have a template for some of these aspects:

- **General course information:** name and number of course, location and time it meets

- **Course goals:** learning goals for the course (the objectives) which should directly relate to your course assignments and readings

- **List of material:** required and optional resources

- **University policies:** issues such as plagiarism, course absences, and disability access

- **Overall course-specific policies:** how you intend to address late assignments, attendance, and incompletes

- **Grading policies:** what counts to "participation" in your course, your approach to grading, the actual point breakdown for As, Bs, etc.

- **Descriptions of assignments:** sometimes instructors wait until the assignment due dates are closer to provide detailed instructions so as

15

not to overwhelm students, but a brief description of each assignment can be helpful.

15-WEEK COURSE SCHEDULE

1. **Introductions.** Discuss course goals, grading, workplace versus academic communication, teamwork, ethics, and global communications. Read Chapter 1, Chapter 2, and pages 182--191 in Chapter 10 (memos). Complete the Team Application in Chapter 1.

2. **Designing, Delivering, and Structuring Information.** Read Chapter 4 and Chapter 5. Set up your interview of a professional in your field about the role of communication in their work. As part of your interview, consider the issues raised in last week's Chapter 2 exercise in the "Computer and Web-Based Application" section.

3. **Researching and Summarizing.** Read Chapter 3 and Chapter 14. Skim Appendix A. Complete the Computer/Web-Based Application in Chapter 3 with a team.

DUE: Interview Summary

4. **Using Effective Style and Design.** Read Chapter 6 and Chapter 8. Complete one of the Diagnostics in the Grammar section of MyTechCommLab™. Use the results to focus on reading in the style and grammar areas that seem to give you the most trouble. Complete the document design evaluation with a partner described in the General Application exercise in Chapter 8.

DUE: Issue and client description for Formal Report Project

5. **Creating Visuals, Writing Proposals.** Read Chapter 7 and Chapter 17. Complete the Visual Rhetoric Tutorial in the Document Design area of the MyTechCommLab™ site. Complete Exercise 1 in the General Applications area of Chapter 7.

6. **Definitions, Descriptions, and Instructions.** Read Chapter 11, Chapter 12, and Chapter 13. Review the teamwork material in Chapter 2. Define team roles on your group instructions assignment. Complete peer reviews of proposals.

DUE: Draft of proposal for peer review. The proposal should be addressed to your "client" describing how you plan to research the issue of interest to them to complete your Formal Report Project at the end of the class. Include your research strategies and key research questions and your timeline for completing the research, analysis, and writing by the final due date at the end of class.

7. **In-Class User Testing Lab**. User-test, group-written instructions and work in groups to plan revisions.

DUE: Revised Proposal

8. **Digital Media and Presentations.** Read all of the chapters on digital communication, Chapters 18–20. Complete the General Application exercise in Chapter 19 and the General/Web-Based Application in Chapter 20.

DUE: Final group-written instructions, and individually written to instructor reflecting on group process

9. **Informal Reports**. Read Chapter 15. View additional examples of Progress Reports under the "Reports" heading of the Model Documents section of MyTechCommLab™.

DUE: Progress Report on Formal Report Project

10. **Employment Materials**. Read Chapter 9. Complete Exercises 1 and 2. Peer review résumé and cover letter from Exercises 1 and 2.

11. **Formal Reports.** Chapter 16. View an example of a Feasibility Report under the "Reports" heading of the Model Documents section of MyTechCommLab™.

Review Appendix A for documentation strategies. View.

DUE: Revised Résumé and Cover Letter

12. **Oral Reports.** Read Chapter 21. Sign up for oral presentation slots.

13. **Oral Reports.**

<u>DUE: Oral Reports.</u> Each student presents a 7–10 minute summary of their Formal Report with at least one visual aid. Review. Peers provide feedback on oral reports.

14. **Oral Reports.** Each student presents a 7–10 minute summary of their Formal Report with at least one visual aid. Letters, Chapter 10. Peers provide feedback on oral reports. Peer review drafts of Formal Report.

<u>DUE: Oral Reports.</u> Review Chapter 14, pages 279–287 (Special Types of Summaries). Each student presents a 7–10 minute summary of their Formal Report with at least one visual aid.

<u>DUE: Draft peer review of Formal Report</u>

15. **Course Wrap-Up.**

<u>DUE: Final Formal Report with front matter, end matter, and letter of transmittal</u>

11-WEEK COURSE SCHEDULE

1. **Introduction to Workplace Writing and Technical Communication.** Discuss course goals, grading, workplace versus academic communication, teamwork, ethics, and global communications. Read Chapter 1, Chapter 2, and pages 182–191 in Chapter 10 (memos). Complete the Team Application in Chapter 1.

2. **Designing, Delivering, and Structuring Information.** Read Chapter 4 and Chapter 5. Set up your interview of a professional in your field about the role of communication in their work. As part of your interview, consider the issues raised in last week's Chapter 2 exercise in the "Computer and Web-Based Application" section.

3. **Researching and Summarizing.** Read Chapter 3 and Chapter 14. Skim Appendix A. Complete the Computer/Web-Based Application in Chapter 3 with a team.
DUE: Interview Summary

4. **Using Effective Style and Design**. Read Chapter 6 and Chapter 8. Complete one of the Diagnostics in the Grammar section of MyTechCommLab™. Use the results to focus on reading in the style and grammar areas that seem to give you the most trouble. Complete the document design evaluation with a partner described in the General Application exercise in Chapter 8.

DUE: Issue and client description for Formal Report Project

5. **Creating Visuals, Writing Proposals**. Read Chapter 7 and Chapter 17. Complete the Visual Rhetoric Tutorial in the Document Design area of the MyTechCommLab™ site. Complete Exercise 1 in the General Applications area of Chapter 7.

DUE: Draft of proposal for peer review. The proposal should be addressed to your "client" describing how you plan to research the issue of interest to them to complete the your Formal Report Project at the end of the class. Include your research strategies and key research questions and your timeline for completing the research, analysis, and writing by the final due date at the end of class.

6. **Definitions, Descriptions, and Instructions**. Read Chapter 11, Chapter 12, and Chapter 13. Review the teamwork material in Chapter 2. Define team roles

19

on your group instructions assignment. In the next week, the team tests and revises the instructions. Complete peer reviews of proposals.

DUE: Revised Proposal

7. **Digital Media and Presentations.** Read all of the chapters on digital communication, Chapters 18–20. Complete the General Application exercise in Chapter 19 and the General/Web-Based Application in Chapter 20.

DUE: Final group-written instructions, and individually written to instructor reflecting on group process.

8. **Informal and Formal Reports**. Read Chapter 15 and Chapter 16. View additional examples of Progress Reports under the "Reports" heading of the Model Documents section of MyTechCommLab™. View an example of a Feasibility Report under the "Reports" heading of the Model Documents section of MyTechCommLab™. Review Appendix A for documentation strategies.

DUE: Progress Report on Formal Report Project

9. **Oral Reports.** Read Chapter 21. Sign up for oral presentation slots.

10. **Oral Reports.** Each student presents a 7–10 minute summary of their Formal Report with at least one visual aid. Letters, Chapter 10. Peers provide feedback on oral reports. Peer review drafts of Formal Report.

DUE: Oral Reports. Review Chapter 14, pages 279–287 (Special Types of Summaries). Each student presents a 7–10 minute summary of their Formal Report with at least one visual aid.

DUE: Draft peer review of Formal Report.

11. **Course Wrap-Up**.

DUE: Final Formal Report with front matter, end matter, and letter of transmittal

CHAPTER 1

Introduction to Technical Communication

This chapter helps distinguish academic writing from technical writing, creating a context for the entire textbook (and your course). From the start, the chapter emphasizes the applied nature of technical communication, meeting the needs of specific people in a particular context.

This chapter also presents key characteristics of effective technical communication that use words and visual design in a range of contexts (paper-based, digital media, and oral presentations). Together, these strategies help accomplish one or more purposes: to inform, instruct, or persuade.

Sometimes, students are initially confused by the word "technical" in "technical communication" and mistakenly believe that if they are not in the technical fields, they do not need to be concerned with this type of writing. By describing a wide range of technical documents, this chapter helps students understand that technical communication is something they will likely encounter and create every day in one form or another.

The chapter also focuses on the process of creating technical communication, emphasizing that most workplace communication is created by teams rather than individuals. As the document takes shape and develops into the final draft, proofreading is an essential step to ensure that the reader does not become distracted and the writer does not look careless. The text presents a range of proofreading strategies that students can apply throughout the course.

After reading this chapter, students will be able to

- Define technical communication
- See how people at work create technical communication
- List the three primary purposes of technical documents

21

- Recognize typical technical communication documents
- Understand the importance of proofreading a document

TEACHING TIPS

To help students understand that this is not just another composition course, spend time discussing the differences between technical and nontechnical writing. You can use a group brainstorming technique to record the commonalities and differences.

Orienting Students to the Essential Role of Technical Writing

Motivation and attitude are crucial in getting students to improve their communication skills. You can engage them by discussing their experience with frustrating instructions, manuals, and such, and ask them to describe how they would have improved the documents. Another approach is to ask students what role communication plays in their future profession and how that communication affects what they can achieve in their future profession. A construction management student, for example, will realize that writing is a key skill to creating effective bids to gain contracts. Students who expect to work in the nonprofit field may say that writing grant proposals will help get money to fund important projects that affect the community and may supply the funding for their own jobs. A future marketer may talk about the role of Web sites in motivating customers to buy. The key in this discussion is to emphasizing the benefits of effective communication in their own fields.

Exploring Audience and Purpose—A Short Writing Exercise

As an initial exercise that shows how audience and purpose affect communication decisions, give students 5 minutes to imagine an audience and purpose regarding the same object and to write with this in mind (e.g. a dollar bill, a plant, a pencil). Tell the students that they will be sharing this orally with another classmate. Have them pair up and share what they've written. Ask the listener to infer the characteristics of the audience and the purpose of the communication. Then, have the writer share their intended audience and purpose (inform, instruct, or persuade). How has the language been adjusted to accomplish the goal with that audience in mind? Have them talk with each other, then share with the class what they learned from this exercise. In Unit 4, audience and purpose are covered in much more detail.

22

Emphasizing the Importance of Peer Review and Proofreading

The chapter's emphasis on proofreading is an opening for a number of in-class discussions. You might ask students how they are affected as readers when they see a document that has spelling errors or typos. What does this indicate about the writer's credibility? How well can they concentrate on the message? In their own writing, you might also see what kind of proofreading habits they have developed. What works well? The proofreading discussion is a good segue into a discussion of peer review and group writing, as proofreading is a step in the process. You will want to emphasize that peer review initially should focus on the broader issues of content and focus, for example, rather than sentence-level proofreading issues. In Chapter 2, the distinction between reviewing and editing is introduced, but you might want to bring this up here as well.

In the realm of proofreading, issues of grammar and punctuation can be challenging to address. The predominance of research has shown that it is most effective for students to learn about these issues in the context of their own writing rather than through drill exercises. To this end, you might want to encourage students to pay attention to recurring issues in their own writing by creating their own personalized Grammar/Style Guide that includes examples of errors and corrected versions from their own writing, along with a related rule that they might draw from Appendix B, which covers grammar, punctuation, mechanics, usage, etc.

ADDITIONAL EXERCISES

1. **Technical Communication in the Workplace Interview**. To help you gather information about the types and importance of communication in organizations, set up a ½-hour interview with someone in a position that is similar to the one you would like to have in three to five years and then write a 1–2 page summary report that highlights the most interesting aspects of the interview. This will help you find out about the value and importance of effective oral and written communication skills in your organization. Example questions include

   - How important are good communication skills (e.g., reading, writing, speaking, and listening) to your professional position?

   - How much of your time each week do you spend on technical or problem-solving activities?

- How much of your time do you spend writing? How much of your time do you spend working with materials written by others?

- How much of your time do you spend in oral communication activities—meetings, interviews, giving assignments to others, making presentations?

- How important are intercultural communications to your professional success? What is your definition of intercultural communications?

- Do you work on projects or assignments alone or as part of a team? How are duties and responsibilities allocated in a team effort?

- Who are the various audiences of the reports or memos that you write? How much do these audiences know about what you do on a daily basis? What kinds of information do they need from your reports and memos? How will different audiences use your reports and memos?

- What types of writing do you do most frequently (e.g., email, interoffice memos, letters, filling out forms, proposals, feasibility reports, progress reports, trip reports, formal reports, and other activities)?

- What is the role of research in your writing? How do you obtain accurate information as the basis for your documents? (e.g., conversations with co-workers, company documents, outside documents)

- Of these, which types of writing have the biggest potential impact on your organization?

2. **Read-Aloud Proofreading Strategy**. Find a paper you have completed for a class or a document you have completed for work. Read the paper aloud, word by word. What errors did you catch? You will likely find that this strategy helps you avoid skimming your own work and catch key errors you might otherwise skip by. In a short paragraph, share your results with your instructor.

3. **Web Proofreading Resources.** In groups of 3–4, develop a list of the top 5 Web resources that have helpful information to help with proofreading. Share this list with the class, along with an annotation that indicates what is particularly helpful about each site. This annotated list will be compiled and distributed (perhaps through a class Web site) for reference throughout the semester.

CHAPTER 1 QUIZ

Indicate whether the statements are TRUE or FALSE by writing T or F in the blank.

1. ___Technical communication rarely focuses on the author's personal thoughts or feelings.

2. ___Technical documents are almost always designed for expert readers.

3. ___Phone calls, conversations, and meetings have largely replaced the need for written documents.

4. ___Most technical writing is done in teams.

5. ___All documents have some persuasive aspect.

6. ___Research is involved in creating virtually all technical documents.

7. ___Technical communication includes digital media such as blogging and PowerPoint slides.

8. ___In the United States, most people read documents from beginning to end.

In items 9 through 11, choose the letter of the expression that best completes the statement.

9. ___Technical communication seeks to (a) anticipate and answer questions (b) help people perform a task, (c) persuade people to do something, (e) all of the above.

10. ___When proofreading your work (a) do so early on in the writing process so you don't have to rework your sentences later, (b) read your paper on a computer screen for easy viewing and correcting, (c) be sure to read the entire document at one time, (d) never rely on computerized writing aids.

11. What are three ways in which technical communication differs from academic communication?

12. What are four different types of technical communication documents?

CHAPTER 2

Teamwork, Ethics, Persuasion, and Global Issues in Technical Communication

This chapter continues discussions briefly touched upon in Chapter 1, providing more in-depth examples and strategies for working effectively in teams, being aware of and practicing ethical communication, being able to persuade others, and being aware of global issues. While many technical communication texts separate these issues into separate chapters, here they are presented together, because these issues are decidedly intertwined in practice. In team-created projects, the process of developing a work product for an audience requires the work team to work together, and communicate with each other. Most work teams are intercultural and often distributed across regions and even countries. Moving team projects forward also involves within-team persuasion, negotiating differences among team members and persuading and motivating others in the team. Creating action among team members also needs to be tempered with the need to do so in an ethical manner.

After reading this chapter, students will be able to

- Organize and manage a team project
- Run a successful meeting
- Identify and manage team conflicts
- Review and edit the work of others on a team
- Recognize and avoid ethical abuses in technical communication
- Effectively persuade your readers
- Understand that technical communication is used by international audiences

TEACHING TIPS

Group Process

Many students have had negative experiences with working in teams, sometimes experiencing conflicts within teams or encountering team members who do not follow through on commitments. So, right from the start, it's important to discuss the value of working in teams—preferably from the students' experience, whether as part of a school project or at work. Continuing the Chapter 1 theme of distinguishing between academic writing and technical communication, you might note the ongoing nature of business relationships and the role of teamwork in that process. Unlike class teams, which generally involve students who may not ever see each other again, work teams involve individuals who will likely collaborate on many different projects over time. One of the key outcomes of effective teamwork today is the ability to leverage the relationships and skills of team members in a future project or opportunity.

You might also ask students to generate their own list of strategies for working on a team project. They will find that many of the strategies presented in the book ring true from their own experience. For their most successful team processes, ask why they think it worked so well. For the less positive team experiences, ask them for the lessons learned for the future. This last question helps them shift from focusing on the negative and instead orient their thinking toward what it takes to create effective teams. This is a helpful discussion to have in smaller groups, with each group generating their own list of top strategies for working successfully in teams and reporting back to the class.

Refer to the General Teaching Tips chapter of this instructor's manual for specific suggestions on how to design effective team projects.

Peer Review

As with teamwork, students also often have negative experiences with the peer review process, mostly because they have not been guided properly in previous experiences. You can help by modeling the strategies described for effectively reviewing and editing the work of others by bringing in a sample piece of writing and working through a peer review process as a class together. Emphasizing the difference between reviewing and editing is important so that students don't get hung up on grammar and spelling issues without addressing the content, organization, design, and style issues first. Reiterate this as they enter into any

30

peer review processes for class assignments. Using a sample document, invite students to focus on the "big picture" feedback first. Watch that they are using the appropriate tone and specificity in their comments on these larger issues. Then, you can focus on the sentence level issues, showing students how to comment on these issues without replacing or correcting every grammar, punctuation, or usage issue.

Ethics

In the area of ethics, you might delve further into the fact that what is legal may not be what is ethical. Exaggerating claims in advertisement is usually legal but arguably unethical. Ask students to provide examples of situations where they or others in their circle have been faced with a potentially unethical, but still legal, choice about doing or saying something, or NOT doing or saying something. Discuss the pressures that might lead a person to take the less ethical path. Students might feel uncomfortable being identified with these scenarios, so one way to increase participation in presenting the scenarios is to invite anonymous submissions via note cards (or anonymous online postings) that could then be distributed to different groups for discussion.

Persuasion

The chapter introduces the concept of persuasion as having three parts – a claim, an interpretation, and a call to action. Where students often fall short is in the interpretation aspect. They will try to jump from the claim to the call to action without helping the reader understand the meaning of the claim. To help students see how the writer helps interpret information, providing meaning to the audience, you might use examples from reports (a preview of later work they will be doing in the class, as well) that draw conclusions from findings. By interpreting the data in a report, the author helps the reader understand why they should care and, ultimately, why the call to action (recommendations in a report) makes sense.

Global and Cultural Issues

You'll notice that cross-cultural issues are woven throughout this chapter, not just in the Global Issues section. This is an important point to explore with students—the key role of cross-cultural communication in the global economy and pluralistic work team environment. Learning how cultural similarities and differences is a critical skill in developing appropriate context and audience specific communication strategies.

As mentioned in the text, cultural considerations include not only global issues but also other potential culture issues such as racial an ethnic groups, religious or spiritual views, sexual orientation, physical ability, etc. Even within the United States, there are definite regional differences in culture. A Minnesotan working on a team with a New Yorker, for example, will find very different regional communication styles. Even within a state, rural and urban cultural differences impact communication. Since most classes include people from a range of geographical locations, this is often a good place to start—inviting students to speak from their own experience of regional differences and similarities.

ADDITIONAL EXERCISES

1. Exploring Ethical Dilemmas. This chapter offered a number of strategies for avoiding ethical abuses. Consider the following situations and come prepared to discuss what action you would take. How might you apply the strategies from the text to the cases here? Be prepared to discuss these with your classmates.

   - You have been authorized to hire a technical assistant, so you are about to prepare an advertisement. This is a time of threatened cutbacks for your company. People hired as "temporary," however, have never seemed to work out well. Should your ad include the warning that this position could only be temporary?

   - You are marketing director for a major importer of coffee beans. Your testing labs report that certain African beans contain roughly twice the caffeine of South American varieties. Many of these African varieties are big sellers, from countries whose coffee bean production helps prop up otherwise desperate economies. Should your advertising of these varieties inform the public about the high caffeine content? If so, how much emphasis should this fact be given?

   - You are a research director for a biotechnology company working on an AIDS vaccine. At a national conference, a researcher from a competing company secretly offers to sell your company crucial data that could speed discovery of an effective vaccine. Should you accept the offer?

2. Meeting Evaluation. Attend a meeting and observe the group dynamics. To what extent does this meeting apply the strategies for organizing, managing, and running a meeting? Write a short report that evaluates how well the meeting seems to follow those strategies and indicates how the meeting dynamics might have been improved.

3. Codes of Ethics. In groups, use the Internet to research one or more codes of ethics from your professional areas of interest. What are similarities and differences you notice in the codes within each profession? What are similarities and differences you notice across the professions represented in your group? What do they reveal about the kinds of pressures that workers experience in each of these professions? Be prepared to discuss your findings with the class as a whole.

4. Exploring Different Perspectives. Through your personal connections or through an international student center on your campus, locate a student from a geographical and cultural background other than yours. In an hour interview, explore at least three of the concepts from the chapter such as

- gender dynamics
- nonverbal (body) language
- perceptions of time
- quicker, more direct decision-makings vs more methodical, longer processes of decision-making
- willingness to question or disagree with others
- attitudes toward oral versus written communication
- value on intuition and ambiguity versus hard evidence/data
- attention to the personal relationships as well as the business relationships

Prepare a 5 minute presentation that highlights key discoveries from your interview about the similarities and differences between your own culture and that of your interviewee.

33

5. Motivating Workplace Compliance: Either in your own workplace or in a workplace you observe, how do workplace communications try to persuade workers to take a particular action? Analyze one of the communications – an email, a memo, a notice, etc.—to see which of the three strategies are being applied: a power connection, a relationship connection, and/or a rational connection? How effective do you think this persuasive approach is? How might the message be even more persuasive? Write a 1–2 page report of your analysis and evaluation.

CHAPTER 2 QUIZ

Indicate whether the statements 1 through 8 are TRUE or FALSE by writing T or F in the blank.

1. ___In collaborating to produce a document, all members of a collaborative team participate in the actual "writing."

2. ___"Reviewing" is a more precise term for "editing."

3. ___ Using pleasurable images to downplay the negative messages of written text may be persuasive, but it is unethical.

4. ___The relationship connection is particularly important in cross-cultural communication.

5. ___Paying attention to "face saving" is key to working across cultures.

6. ___Any technical document may be distributed globally.

7. ___Face-to-face meetings are still essential for personal contact.

8. ___ Women who speak up in meetings are often perceived as overbearing, while men who do so are considered to be leadership-oriented.

In items 9 through 10, choose the letter of the expression that best completes the statement.

9. ___Sources of conflict in collaborative groups include (a) interpersonal differences, (b) cultural differences, (c) gender differences, (d) all of these, (e) b and c.

10. ___The preferred strategy is to use (a) the power connection strategy, (b) the rational connection strategy, (c) the relationship connection strategy, (d) b and c, (e) a and b.

35

Additional Fill-In the Blank and Short Answer Questions

11. The three elements of persuasive appeals are _____, _____, and _____.

12. What are four different virtual collaboration strategies you might use in your own profession, and how might each be useful to you?

CHAPTER 3

The Research Process in Technical Communication

This chapter focuses on critically evaluating research sources, whether they are primary or secondary, online or in print. The chapter engages students in becoming a savvy consumer of research resources, weighing advantages and disadvantages of different sources and applying a balanced approach to research that applies different types of sources as well as varying perspectives.

After reading this chapter, students will be able to

- Apply critical thinking in your research
- Understand the difference between primary and secondary research
- Locate the Web-based and hard-copy secondary sources you need
- Consult primary sources via inquiries, informational interviews and surveys, observations, and experiments

TEACHING TIPS

While students may have an initial plan for how to conduct their research, they also need to realize that, as the chapter discusses, one source of information will lead to others, and that new questions will arise, leading to additional research. At its core, research is a nonlinear, recursive process that involves rethinking along the way. What may seem like an essential question at the beginning of the project may prove to be a much less important issue than another once they get further into the research process. Acknowledging shifting nature of the research process in the earlier weeks of the semester will help your prepare your students for surprises and shifts in their own projects.

Hands-On Research Labs

If you are teaching a face-to-face course, try to schedule access to a computer lab the week you cover these research issues. Since so much secondary research occurs online now, either through online databases through universities or through Web search engines and indexes, it is valuable to use hands-on exercises to involve students in different research strategies with your coaching at hand. Commonly, students today are used to one research strategy—a quick search of Google. Few students are aware of more advanced search features of Google, let alone the reality of a wide variety of other search engines and indexes, so it is important to let them see the value and potential limitations of different search tools.

Linking Research Strategies to Class Assignments

You might use this chapter as a jumping off point for students to begin to identify potential research strategies to complete a semester-long project. Having students specify potential primary and secondary sources early on, and critically evaluate the strengths and weaknesses of their sources, will help them build a balanced, more complete project at the end of the semester. In addition, you might want to include a peer-review component to the research strategy, considering the strengths and potential weaknesses of the sources according to the strategies posed in this chapter's materials. What are the potential biases of the sources proposed? What additional sources might help the researcher consider additional important viewpoints?

Creating a Research Community Through Collaborative Online Tools

This chapter points to wikis and blogs as sources of information when conducting research. These tools are addressed in more detail as genres of writing in Chapter 18. You might also incorporate these tools in your class experience by designating groups to be experts on particular topics of interest regarding technical communication such as visual design, international communication, ethics, etc. Each group could create a wiki site or a blog that shares the results of their research about that topic and leads other students to helpful resources in this area. This would encourage ongoing exploration and a sense of ownership over key course concepts.

ADDITIONAL EXERCISES

1. **Evaluating a Feedback Strategy**. At a local business or mall, participate in an opportunity to provide user feedback on a product or service. Write a 1-2 page evaluation of the design. What was effective? How might it have been improved?

2. **Comparing the Value of Web Sites**. Assume that as communications director for XYZ, an international corporation, you oversee intercultural training of native U.S. employees who will be working in various company branches worldwide and collaborating routinely with members of different cultures. To enhance employee training, you decide to compile a short list of Web sites that provide up-to-date information on various cultures.

   Find at least five sites that your company might use as resources. Provide a brief description of each, and rank the sites in terms of the depth of information each provides on a given culture (e.g. Pakistani, Saudi Arabian, etc.). In a memo to all employees, recommend which site(s) to visit for general or specific information and for certain types of information (history, behaviors, values, etc.).

   An example of a cite might be the CIA World Factbook Online at shttps://www.cia.gov/library/publications/the-world-factbook/

3. **Designing an Online Questionnaire**. Given the convenience and speed of using Web-based surveys, companies are increasingly using them as a method of delivering questionnaires. Explore online questionnaire design by using one of the free online survey tools available on the Web to complete this exercise. Search for "free Web survey" to find online survey tools and pick one for your group to try out for this exercise.

   Your group is a marketing team that works for a vending machine company trying to decide which products to stock at your campus. You will design a questionnaire to help gain critical information from your target audience— college students.

   - Design a 10-question survey that will help you answer this research question. Be sure that you apply the Strategies for Surveys from your textbook, including an engaging introduction that provides appropriate information as well as a well-constructed set of questions.

- Send your classmates the link to your survey so that they can complete it.

- After reviewing the results, consider how you would interpret the data you have gathered. What conclusions might you draw from this data? What additional resources or questions would you want to explore having looked at this data? What new connections or possibilities are revealed by these results?

- Consider the survey design process. As you looked at the surveys created by the other groups, what differences did you notice? Would you have made any changes to your own survey based on what you saw in the other surveys?

- Prepare a 1 page report to the head of the marketing department of XYZ Vending Company stating your survey results, your conclusions, further areas of research, and any changes to the questionnaire you would recommend before distributing it to the larger student population.

4. **Comparing Online Search Tools**. In small groups of 3–4, experiment with at least four different search tools including two subject directories and two search engines.

Part 1. Using the same key word searches, compare the first five hits from each search tool. What differences do you notice?

- types of sources listed (articles, blog postings, advertisements)

- publishers of sources listed (educational, commercial, personal)

- relevancy to your topic

- timeliness

Part 2. Now, try using any advanced search features that you might have available in each of these tools. For example, many advanced features allow you to narrow your search by date or by sponsor (.gov or .com). You might also be able to exclude sites that contain particular words or that include only particular file types (e.g. Word documents).

40

Part 3. Having explored various aspects of these search tools and the kinds of results you obtain from them, what advice can you offer your peers regarding these tools? Prepare a brief presentation. If your classroom has an online computer and projector, show examples that illustrate your main points.

CHAPTER 3 QUIZ

Indicate whether the statements 1 through 7 are TRUE or FALSE by writing T or F in the blank.

1. ___A survey is an example of secondary research.

2. ___Subject directories are indexes of information that are maintained by computer programs.

3. ___Sometimes the most reliable material resides in less attractive, text-only sites.

4. ___Commercial sites should not be used as reliable sources of information since they are inherently biased.

5. ___Blogs can be sources of relevant and reliable information.

6. ___Questionnaires use closed-ended questions, not open-ended questions.

7. ___Direct observation is the surest way to eliminate bias in research.

In items 8 through 10, choose the letter of the expression that best completes the statement.

8. ___Thinking critically about research depends on all of the following except (a) finding a definite answer, (b) looking at the research from many viewpoints, (c) achieving sufficient depth, (d) asking the right questions, (e) evaluating the reliability and completeness of sources.

9. ___Sources that explore topics at deeper levels include (a) newspapers, (b) tabloids, (c) commercial Web sites, (d) popular press, (e) trade publications.

10. ___Informational interviews (a) do not require a clear purpose statement because they are exploratory in nature, (b) should avoid providing questions in advance to create a more spontaneous and authentic reaction, (c) should use open-ended questions instead of

closed-ended questions (d) should always be taped, (e) should get the most sensitive questions out of the way from the start.

Additional Fill-In the Blank and Short Answer Questions

11. What are examples of "gray literature" in your field of interest?

12. With the speed and convenience of online surveys, in what situation might you want to use a mailed survey instead?

CHAPTER 4

Designing and Delivering Usable Information

This chapter introduces the importance of considering who the audience is, how they will be using the document, the purpose of the communication, as well as a range of other important factors such as the budget, setting, and timing. Through careful consideration of these elements, a writer can develop an effective plan for how to approach a communication task. Despite a well-reasoned approach to a writing task, however, a specific approach can still be ineffective. For this reason, user testing is another key element discussed here. Gaining feedback from potential users can help identify areas that need revising. The chapter briefly discusses five key areas that respondents might have difficulties with: content; organization; style; layout and visuals; and ethical, legal, and cultural considerations. These areas are discussed in greater detail in subsequent chapters.

After reading this chapter, students will be able to

- Define usability
- Analyze a document's audience (primary and secondary, relationship to them, technical background, cultural background)
- Determine a document's purpose (primary and secondary, intended use)
- Create a task analysis for a document (main task and subtasks)
- Consider a document's setting, potential problems, length, format, timing, and budget
- Develop an information plan for a document
- Visualize the stages of writing, testing, and revising a document

TEACHING TIPS

Instilling an Audience Perspective

For many students, particularly those who do not have extensive work experience, writing is still viewed from the academic lens, as a transfer of information from the brain to the page. The shift to reader-centered writing can feel uncomfortable at first. To help instill this new perspective, you can incorporate the Audience and Purpose Profile Sheet (Figure 4.1 of the text) into in-class exercises as well as your assignments. You might also consider having students complete a more extensive Information Plan (Figure 4.2 of the text) for one or more assignments. Students would submit an accompanying memo that describes the audience, purpose, and other key considerations relative to that particular writing task. Tell students you will read and evaluate their writing as their intended audience would. You might, for example, assume the viewpoint of a supervisor from the student's workplace considering the proposal. This approach enables students to write to a workplace audience (such as their supervisor) as the intended audience rather than a professor as the intended audience.

Reverse Engineering Documents

You might also use reverse-engineering approach to a document. You can have students analyze a document in class and determine what type of audience, purpose, and other considerations influenced writing and design decisions related to the sample document.

Addressing the Issue of Document Length

Students invariably ask, "How long should this assignment be?" as they try to apply versions of the "500-word essay" formula to all assignments. This question is your cue to remind students of creating audience-focused communications. Invite them to think of what key factors would influence this decision. How long does it take to meet the audience's needs? What will it take to answer all of the audience's potential questions? How much information is enough, and how much is too much? How might the setting in which the audience is using the document affect the potential length? How might budgetary considerations affect a document's length?

ADDITIONAL EXERCISES

1. **Evaluating Usability**. The registrar of your school is considering re-designing the university catalog to better meet student needs. In groups of 3–4, determine three tasks a student user might want to accomplish by using the university catalog. For example, one task might be to find out what the required courses are for a particular major. User-test the catalog by trying to perform each of the three tasks. Evaluate the document's effectiveness in helping you accomplish these three tasks. In particular, evaluate what works well and what might need some adjustments in the areas of

   - content

   - organization

   - style

   - layout and visuals

   - ethical, legal, and cultural considerations

   Develop a 1–2 page memo to the registrar that recommends changes to the catalog design based on your findings.

2. **Analyzing International Web Sites**. This could be either a group or an individual exercise. Go to a Web site of a multinational corporation such as IBM, Starbucks, McDonalds, or Pizza Hut that includes links to country-specific Web site options.

   - Find the country-specific sites for three English-speaking countries. Looking at these sites, what strategies have these sites used to connect with their intended audiences? What similarities and differences do you notice? What can you surmise about the intended audiences of each site? How have the cultural dimensions of these countries influenced the company's approach to creating each of the sites?

   - Now, expand your comparison to two countries where English is not the dominant language. Just looking at the visual layout and images, what cultural influences assumptions have been made in the designs?

   Share your findings with the class.

47

3. **Re-Designing for User Needs**. Consider a paper you have written for another class. Who was your primary audience for that assignment? Likely, this was your professor. Now, consider a different audience who you might be interested in some aspect of this information. Examples could include, for example, a friend, a co-worker, an elementary school teacher, a niece or nephew, or someone else. Develop an information plan for a revised document that would meet the needs of this new audience and your new purpose.

CHAPTER 4 QUIZ

Indicate whether the statements 1 through 7 are TRUE or FALSE by writing T or F in the blank.

1. ___The relationship of the writer to the reader does not affect how to approach a writing situation.

2. ___Audience analysis is necessary only when a document is long or complex.

3. ___Both the primary and secondary purpose of a document affect the language, format, and other features.

4. ___Information needs may be culturally determined.

5. ___Write all documents at the technical level of laypeople.

6. ___The target audience and the specific audience may be different.

7. ___Across cultures, readers prefer a direct, plain language approach to communication.

In items 8 through 10, choose the letter of the expression that best completes the statement.

8. ___A task analysis (a) entails knowing what the audience needs to do to accomplish something, (b) applies only when creating instructions or procedures, (c) uses noun phrases to express the steps, (d) is a process used primarily in technical fields, (e) none of the above.

9. ___An information plan (a) includes a purpose statement, (b) should be kept to 1-page or less, (c) avoids issues related to budget, (d) describes potential problems (e) a and d.

10. ___ "General readers" (a) do not exist, so don't try writing to them, (b) want high levels of detail to fully understand the message, (c) want explanations to accompany facts (d) want you to show

them how smart you are, (e) prefer to know the theoretical basis of the topic at hand.

Additional Fill-In the Blank and Short Answer Questions

11. If you were to create a set of instructions for how to make coffee drinks for a local coffee house, how might the setting affect the way in which you approach writing the document?

12. What are five aspects of a document that you might want to ask user testers about in order to determine how you should revise the document?

CHAPTER 5

Structuring Information for Your Readers

While the first four chapters of the text focus on the foundation of technical communication, this chapter, and chapters 6–8 focus how to insure that documents hold together well—what the text refers to as a set of *blueprints*. Chapter 5 delves into ways of structuring documents so that readers can follow the writer's thinking and easily grasp the information. Subsequent chapters address issues of style, visuals, and design.

The intention of this chapter is to show that a well-organized document doesn't just *happen* –it evolves from a careful plan. Chapter 5 guides students through a progression of thinking through the larger organizational structure, followed by successively more detailed organizational strategies. To start, the overarching structure of most documents includes an introduction, body, and conclusion. The writer then needs to break the body down into digestible units, chunks based on the writer's needs and the document's purpose. The next step is to order the chunks logically (spatial, chronological, problem-solution, or cause-effect) depending upon the content and type of document. One way to conceptualize the overall relationship between these chunks of information is to use an outline as a planning tool to lay out the document's overall structure and flow. The chapter provides some detailed advice on how to structure an outline well.

With the main chunks ordered and the overall document structure in place, the writer can look at the smaller-scale issues of paragraph structure to make sure that every paragraph includes a topic sentence, every sentence supports that topic sentence, and all of the sentences form a connected line of thought, leading from the topic sentence to a conclusion.

After all of the above elements are in place, the writer can turn to the two final elements addressed in this chapter. First, headings can help provide useful guideposts for the reader throughout the document. Second, for longer documents, an overview at the beginning of the document may be appropriate to provide a brief preview of what writers can expect from the document.

After reading this chapter, students will be able to

- Use a standard or varied introduction/body/conclusion structure
- Create a brief or formal outline
- Chunk the information into discrete units
- Determine the best sequence for the material
- Shape each paragraph for effectiveness
- Create clear headings
- Provide overviews of longer documents

TEACHING TIPS

Because they already have studied decisions about purpose, audience, and content in earlier chapters, students can now appreciate how decisions about organization can help writers connect with their audience. Emphasize to students the reality of busy professionals who have little time and who need to find key pieces of information quickly. From this understanding, they can see how clear organization, chunking of information, and headings can help meet the needs of their audience.

Outlining as a Process

This chapter emphasizes the benefits of outlining to develop the document's structure. Outlining is a valuable skill that comes with practice. As students work through their own outlines and criticize those of others, they begin to see writing as a *process*—a procedure that is deliberate and fully planned – instead of an exercise in which they empty their heads onto the page. Stress that outlines come in all shapes and sizes, and, like building plans for a house, the outline can always be revised as needed. The ordered outline shown in the text represents the *product* of outlining, not the *process*. Beneath any finished outline (or any finished document) lie pages of scribbling and things crossed out, jumbled lists, arrows, and fragments of ideas. Remind students that writing begins in disorder. Messiness is a natural and often essential part of writing in its early stages. By acknowledging this up front, you can help dissipate some of the initial fears and anxiety that students have at the beginning of the writing process.

Focusing on Paragraphs

The bulk of problems with structure and content occur at the paragraph level, especially with paragraphs that are poorly developed or that are disorganized, arbitrary blocks of sentences on a page. Even writers with fluency and imagination often lack basic paragraph logic. The standard paragraph, then, is an appropriate beginning model for strong and weak writers alike. Attention to paragraphs teaches essential features of rhetorical awareness: recognizable beginnings, middles, and endings; clear and distinct main points; convincing support; appropriate amounts of generality and abstraction; unity and coherence. These are features of all discourse, regardless of length. By peer reviewing each other's paragraphs with these features in mind, students can hone not only their paragraphing skills but also their ability to organize entire documents.

ADDITIONAL EXERCISES

1. **Reverse Outlining**. The chapter introduces outlining as a tool for up-front planning of a document. Sometimes, in the writing process, it can be easy to wander from this initial plan. One way to identify potential problems in a paper is to use a tool called reverse outlining. In this process, you check a paper that has already been written by systematically reviewing each of the paragraphs in a document. Try the following with either one of your own papers or with a technical document you locate.

   - On a separate paper, create a number for each paragraph

   - Under each number, state the main point of each paragraph. If there are multiple main points, jot them all down.

   - After you've done this for each paragraph, consider the following:

     o Do any of the paragraphs have too many main ideas that might need to be split up into two or more focused paragraphs?

     o Does each paragraph have a topic sentence, and does each topic sentence actually represent the main idea of the paragraph?

     o Does each sentence in the paragraph help support the main idea of the paragraph?

- Does the order of the main ideas make sense, or would it make sense to reorder parts of the document?

- Does any main idea seem unrelated, unnecessary to the overall purpose of the document—does each paragraph contribute to the unity of the document? (i.e. Should something be dropped?)

- Is anything missing?

Create a set of recommendations for any re-writes that might be appropriate based on the reverse outlining process.

2. **Word Processing Templates**. Word processors include templates for a variety of technical documents—memos, letters, reports, brochures, etc. Choose a template to evaluate. In a short memo, compare and contrast the structure of the template with the guidance provided in this chapter.

3. **The Power of Chunking and Headings**. In groups of 2–3, locate an electronic version of a technical document or a portion of one that is about 3–5 pages in length. Remove any headings included in the document, and lump related paragraphs together so that the document appears to have long stretches of text without a logical breakdown. Send this de-chunked version of the document to another group in your class. Using a similarly de-chunked document given to your group by another, now create appropriate chunks and headings to help break up the document for a reader.

5. **Site Analysis.** Visit 3 different government Web sites and evaluate the effectiveness of each site in structuring the information through chunking, sequencing, paragraphing, headings, and overviews. Write a 1–2 page report evaluating what seemed to be particularly effective and where these sites might have been improved. Compare the sites—where do you see common structural elements that seem particularly effective, and where do they seem to fall short collectively? What audience considerations might have driven the decisions made about organization of these sites?

CHAPTER 5 QUIZ

Indicate whether the statements 1 through 8 are TRUE or FALSE by writing T or F in the blank.

1. ___ Readers of printed pages expect longer passages of text than readers of Web pages.

2. ___ Once the writing process has begun, a working outline never should be changed.

3. ___ In technical writing, the topic sentence usually appears first in the paragraph.

4. ___ Chunking is only relevant for Web-based documents.

5. ___ A progress report usually follows a problem/solution sequence.

6. ___ Transitions and connectors help create a sense of unity in a paragraph.

7. ___ Some documents may not need headings.

8. ___ Overviews are not appropriate for instructions.

In items 9 through 10, choose the letter of the expression that best completes the statement.

9. ___ A conclusion is a good place to (a) take a position (b) make recommendations, (c) suggest further research, (d) add new information, (e) a, b, and c.

10. Formal outlines (a) use letters for the introduction, body, and conclusion, (b) indents the first level sub-topics, (c) must include at least two sub-topics for each level of division, (d) b and c, (e) a and b.

Additional Fill-In the Blank and Short Answer Questions

11. Outlines are organized by _____ notation or _____ notation.

12. Using examples of documents you might create in your own chosen profession, when might it be appropriate to use each of the four sequencing strategies presented in this chapter?

CHAPTER 6

Writing with a Readable Style

This chapter focuses on sentence-level writing issues to help students create effective sentences that meet audience needs. A key message here is that creating powerful sentences requires more than just correct grammar and spelling. It requires strategic choices in four main areas:

1. **writing clearly:** minimizing ambiguities, preferring the active voice and using the passive voice selectively, avoiding nominalizations, reducing modifying nouns, and avoiding unnecessary jargon

2. **writing concisely:** avoiding wordiness and eliminating redundancy and repetition

3. **writing fluently:** combining related ideas, varying sentence construction and length, and using parallel structure

4. **writing personably:** adjusting tone and avoiding sexist and biased language

After reading this chapter, students will be able to

- Recognize that style places the audience's needs first

- Appreciate the important role that style plays in virtually any document

- Use various strategies to write clearly

- Use various strategies to write concisely

- Use various strategies to write fluently

- Use various strategies to write personably

TEACHING TIPS

Using MyTechComm

In addition to the resources and exercises in this chapter, you might consider referring students to the MyTechCommLab online resource. There, students can run through additional exercises in the Grammar and Usage section in the area called the ExerciseZone. To keep with the focus of Chapter 6, you can have them concentrate specifically on the set of exercises on Usage and Style. This tool allows students to practice the skills learned in the chapter and provides instant feedback. If you want to track whether students have completed the exercises, you can have the results emailed to you via this online tool. You also have the option to have students complete a diagnostic to help them identify their strengths and weaknesses, though the diagnostic tool combines both style and grammar issues. The MyTechComm resource is discussed in more detail in the Using MyTechcommLab chapter of this instructor's manual.

Reviewing Style in Context

The most powerful way for students to learn about style issues, though, is to see the overall context of the sentences and how they affect the writing. Therefore, using peer review or review of other writing from outside the class is really the most effective strategy for addressing style issues. The General Application and Team Application exercises provide excellent opportunities for practice – you might bring additional examples into class for students to review. Having students review the same piece of writing and compare their suggestions regarding style can help them realize that one "right" answer may not exist and that a variety of approaches are equally valid, depending upon the goal of the writer and needs of the audience. Students will see that having more than one person review a document can leverage varying perspectives. What one person might see, another may not. On the other hand, the writer may also receive conflicting suggestions—affirming an important point that the writer gets to make the ultimate choices about how to craft the style of a document.

Two Ways of Looking at Wordiness

When you discuss the importance of writing concisely, emphasize that writing can suffer from two kinds of wordiness: one kind occurs when readers receive information they don't need (think of an overly detailed weather report during local television news). The other kind of wordiness occurs when too many words

58

are used to convey information readers do need (e.g. "a great deal of potential for the future" instead of "great potential"). Every word in the document should advance the writer's meaning.

Bringing Style Concerns to the "Real World"

At some point in your discussions with students about the style advice in this chapter, you will likely have a student who says, "All of this advice about style is fine, but I have a boss who writes in flowery or pretentious language and expects employees to do the same." A realistic response to this challenge could be

> If your employer insists on needless jargon or elaborate phrasing, then you have little choice in the matter. Here, we study what is best in matters of style; but what is best is not always what some people consider appropriate. Determine quickly what writing style your employer or organization expects. For short-term necessity, play by the rules; but for a long-term practice, remember that most documents that get superior results are written in plain English.

ADDITIONAL EXERCISES

1. **Plain Language Movement**. Research the phrase "plain language" to find out about efforts at the national level and your own state to help make government documents more readable to the public. Write a 1–2 page report about your findings, including specific examples of successes in this area.

2. **Evaluating Tone**. Identify a Web site that is in an area of interest to you. What is the intended audience for this Web site? How have the creators of the Web site adjusted their tone to reach this audience? What specific strategies related to tone from the chapter do you see reflected in this site? Are there any areas where the tone might have been adjusted to be even more effective? Be prepared to discuss your findings about the site with your classmates (either in an online discussion area, if available, or in a face-to-face discussion).

3. **Rooting out Biased Language**. In earlier chapters, we discussed primary research and the importance of careful wording of questionnaires. Find five written surveys to evaluate for this exercise. How well do they employ

strategies for unbiased language? Where do they fall short, and how might the surveys be rewritten to avoid bias?

CHAPTER 6 QUIZ

Indicate whether the statements 1 through 8 are TRUE or FALSE by writing T or F in the blank.

1. ___ The passive voice should always be avoided.

2. ___Jargon can be useful in communications among specialists.

3. ___Whenever possible, you should preface your assertions with "I think," "In my opinion," "I believe," or some other qualifier.

4. ___Nominalizations add credibility and efficiency to your writing.

5. ___Avoid using short sentences in technical writing.

6. ___Combining sentences can help deemphasize some ideas and emphasize others.

7. ___Using the term "Ms." is an out-of-date strategy that should be avoided.

8. ___Inefficient style is not only difficult to read, but also potentially unethical when it confuses the audience.

In items 9 through 10, choose the letter of the expression that best completes the statement.

9. ___ Sentences using active voice, (a) include a clear agent performing the action, (b) might be too blunt to be effective, (c) might be inappropriate if the object is more important than the subject, d) have the recipient of the action in the subject slot of the sentence, e) a, b and c.

10. ___In choosing the appropriate tone, (a) show confidence and directness by using the active voice, (b) remember that using "you" and "your" is too informal, (c) emphasize the positive, (d) b and c, (e) a and c.

Additional Fill-In the Blank and Short Answer Questions

11. A noun that has been formed from a verb and often ends in *ion* is called a _____ .

12. Reduce the following sentence by at least 10 words:

It is necessary that you take action to complete the reduction of the workload on the staff.

CHAPTER 7

Using Audience Centered Visuals

This chapter discusses visuals as another element that makes up a set of technical blueprints. They help readers interpret and remember complex information, show readers how items look or work, and show readers how items are organized or created. They provide quick, efficient ways for users to access information.

As students consider the different types of visuals presented in the chapter, the chapter guides them in choosing appropriate visuals for the audience and purpose, being careful to avoid unethical representations. It also emphasizes thoughtful choices about the placement, referencing, and design of visuals.

After reading this chapter, students will be able to

- Appreciate the role of visuals in technical communications
- Determine when to use visuals on their own or when to use visuals with text
- Distinguish between different types of visuals
- Understand how to choose visuals appropriately for the audience and their purpose
- Place, cross-reference, and present visuals appropriately for readers
- Use color in visuals
- Appreciate the importance of using visuals in an ethical manner

TEACHING TIPS

Emphasizing the Meaning and Purpose of Visuals

Visuals are an excellent medium for compressing and organizing data. It's important to reiterate that the user should be able to easily understand how the visual relates to the main purpose of the document—why it matters. As mentioned in the chapter, sometimes this is easily identifiable from looking at the visual in context. But, other times, it's important to be more explicit in the accompanying text, and the implications of the data need to be discussed. Using example documents to illustrate, show students samples of different ways in which the text of documents works in tandem with the visuals—how they explain and interpret the visual information and help focus the reader's attention on the most important information.

Utilizing Hands-On Design Labs

If you have access to a computer lab, it can be very helpful for students to have hands-on, guided experience converting raw data into charts, graphs, and tables. Students often do not have this skill and are intimidated when it comes time to create their own—pairing students together for this exercise can help students more familiar with the technological aspects work with those less familiar. After creating their visuals, including a number, title, and label, they can compare the different approaches that each group has taken to designing the visual. Ask students about assumptions they made along the way that drove their design decisions. This kind of meta-cognitive dialogue helps reiterate the importance of choice in the process of designing visuals.

ADDITIONAL EXERCISES

1. **Depicting a Process.** Create a flow chart that depicts your process for planning a party. Use a computer program such as PowerPoint, Word, or another software product to create a clear visual representation. Use color and design elements that help emphasize key elements in the process.

2. **3-D Virtual Visuals.** Except for videos, this chapter focuses on visual representations in 2-dimensional space. Some communicators are experimenting with 3-dimensional representations that allow users to interact with the visuals in virtual space. Search the Web for information on "virtual reality and business" and "virtual globe" for examples of these type

of applications. Find three different examples of 3-dimensional visuals. In a 1–2 page report, describe each of these visual representations and explain what type of purpose and audience might make this an appropriate visual form to use.

3. **Designing for Accessibility**. While color is certainly a powerful tool to use for emphasizing and distinguishing key parts of a visual, over-reliance on color without the use of other contrast techniques can make your visuals difficult, if not impossible, for color-blind people to interpret. In groups of 3–4, use the Internet to research tips on designing for the color blind. Find a visual from a document or Web site to evaluate based on guidelines you have discovered. What works well about the visual regarding meeting the needs of the color blind? What suggestions would you have for revisions to the design to be more effective for this audience? Present your findings to the rest of the class.

4. **Titling**. Locate a graph from a document or online source. Create three possible titles for the visual that might be effective. From a reader's perspective, how do these potential titles compare? Which might be most useful to you and why?

CHAPTER 7 QUIZ

Indicate whether the statements 1 through 7 are TRUE or FALSE by writing T or F in the blank.

1. ___ Distortion for the sake of emphasis is often justified.

2. ___Visuals should always be accompanied by accompanying textual discussion.

3. ___ Tables are appropriate for quantitative information, not qualitative information.

4. ___A chart depicts relationships that are plotted on vertical and horizontal axes.

5. ___Photographs you find on the Web can be used freely.

6. ___Flow charts move from bottom to top, showing the how the process moves up.

7. ___YouTube and similar Web-based video sharing sites are inappropriate for company use.

In items 8 through 10, choose the letter of the expression that best completes the statement.

8. ___ For illustrating a trend, the appropriate figure is typically (a) a table, (b) a pie chart, (c) a photograph, d) a block diagram, (e) a bar graph.

9. ___Organization charts, (a) depict the breakdown of a project, (b) use lines and graphs to show the economic trend of a company, (c) show processes within an organization (d) show a hierarchy of relationships between departments, (e) none of the above.

10. ___Photographs, (a) are always preferable to illustrations if available, (b) can provide too much detail, confusing the user, (c) no longer need professionals to create them since digital photography and photo editing are so easily available, (d) a, b, and c, (e) a and b.

Additional Fill-In the Blank and Short Answer Questions

11. When might you want to use a line graph as opposed to a bar graph?

12. How do illustrations differ from diagrams?

67

CHAPTER 8

Designing User-Friendly Documents

This chapter discusses the final element of technical communication blueprints, the overall appearance of a document to create user-friendly documents guided by the audience and purpose. In general, audiences want the design of the document to be 1) inviting and accessible; 2) work as a single, cohesive unit; 3) form a visual hierarchy; and 4) respect the diversity of its readers.

To meet these four needs of the readers, writers employ a variety of strategies to achieve consistency, cohesiveness, navigation, and emphasis.

> **Elements for Consistency and Cohesiveness:** grid patterns, strategic paragraph lengths, paragraph justification, line spacing, indentation, font style, and font size

> **Design Elements for Navigation and Emphasis:** headings; font styles such as color, shading, bold, italic, and underlining; bulleted and numbered lists; running heads and feet; tables of contents and indexes

After reading this chapter, students will be able to

- Understand the importance of document design
- Appreciate what readers expect from a document's design
- Identify design elements for consistency and coherence
- Use design elements for consistency and coherence
- Use design elements for navigation and emphasis

TEACHING TIPS

Many students tend to regard headings, font style, color, and the like as annoyances or trivialities. Therefore, it is important to emphasize that the reader's first impression of a document is a purely visual, aesthetic judgment. A sloppy format is a sure way to alienate a reader. At a glance, readers can feel overwhelmed by the information, or at ease with their ability to process it. They get a sense of how "professional" it seems, or whether it appears to be thrown together with little thought. The visual design of a document can make the difference between the willingness to look at it now, or a decision set it aside to slog through later (if at all). By effectively using headings, bullets, graphics, color, page layout, and other visual design strategies, we can help our readers find and use the information we provide.

Learning by Example

A key concept here is that user-friendly design emerges from creativity guided by sound design principles (covered in the chapter). To help students explore different design strategies, discuss an array of sample documents with a variety of effective visual design elements. Ask students how these documents reflect the principles learned in the text, but, more importantly, how these documents seem to them as readers—what are the components that feel user-friendly to them? What other options might have been possible?

Experimenting with Formatting Tools

There is not agreement among technical communication professors on the issue of whether or not to address specific software tools in courses, but the reality is that many of our students are unfamiliar with how to implement the design ideas they might have. In particular, they may need some guidance on how to create and format headers and footers, how to work with a word processing program's styles features (and the importance of doing so to make document-wide changes easier), and how to work with lines, boxes, and shading to emphasize particular aspects of the text.

While you might address formatting tools by demonstrating key features from the front of the room, a potentially more effective teaching strategy would be to rely on the wisdom of groups to share their knowledge and learn through the process of doing (with your coaching as needed). One helpful in-class strategy is to provide an electronic version of an unformatted document for students to format

70

and design in groups. By doing this in a computer lab, you can provide technical help along the way if needed. Each group can present their re-designed document and explain their rationale for the design decisions they made. Since all of the students are working on the same document, but in different groups, a comparison of different approaches at the end of this exercise helps students see that there are many ways of approaching the task of creating user-friendly documents.

ADDITIONAL EXERCISES

1. **Style Guide.** For a group-written project in your class, before the group completes the assignment, create a record of document design decisions your team has made about how you will design the document. This will become the guide for drafting the sections of your document in a way that ensures a cohesive, consistent approach.

   Step 1. In a two-column table, create a record of the design technique on one side of the page and the style decisions you have made on the other side of the page.

Document Design Technique	Decisions Made for Consistency
grid patterns	
paragraph justification	
line spacing	
indentation	
overall document font style (type of serif or sans serif font chosen)	
overall document font size	

Heading and sub-heading formatting (include formatting decisions for 3 heading levels)	
Style for bullets and lists	
Running heads and feet	
Other visual elements	

(Exercise adapted from Lay, Mary M. *Technical Communication*. Boston: Irwin/McGraw-Hill, 2000.

2. **Web-Based Collaborative Document Design**. Increasingly, documents are being created via Web-based word processing programs that are often available for free and easily accessible to distributed teams (e.g. Google docs). Compare the document design features available in one of these Web-based tools with those of your own desktop-based software. How would you evaluate the ease and effectiveness of the Web-based option for creating well-designed documents?

3. **Age-Appropriate Design Decisions**. Look for public education materials written on a specific topic but which are available in different formats for different age groups (small children versus adults). Health-related topics, for example, often have materials available for young children and materials available for adults on the same topic (e.g. dental hygiene, healthy food choices, etc.). Compare the visual design strategies used in the documents you find.

- What patterns do you notice about the design decisions made for these documents?

- What assumptions are made about the audience needs, and how have the designs attempted to meet those needs?

- Do you think these assumptions are valid?

Prepare a brief oral presentation to share with a small group of your peers in class.

4. **Evaluating Label Design**. Review the labeling of a painkiller or cold medication. What purpose or purposes does this communication serve, and for whom? How well do the design decisions made serve the audience(s) and purpose(s) you've identified? What design strategies might make this even more effective, given the space limitations that are inherent in a label?

CHAPTER 8 QUIZ

Indicate whether the statements 1 through 7 are TRUE or FALSE by writing T or F in the blank.

1. ___ Page design and structure are synonymous.

2. ___ Usually, readers scan a page quickly to get a sense of the overall readability of a document.

3. ___ A document's design indicates its functionality.

4. ___ Memos or letters follow a horizontal grid pattern.

5. ___ Margins of ½ inch or smaller are desirable for most documents.

6. ___ Serif fonts are appropriate for formal reports.

7. ___ The table of contents should match the headings structure of your document exactly.

   In items 8 through 10, choose the letter of the expression that best completes the statement.

8. ___ Paragraphs in a document (a) should all be about the same length, (b) should be consistently short, (c) should be consistently long, d) should be at least 15 lines long, (e) should vary in length.

9. ___ Unjustified text (a) has uneven spacing between words, (b) is common for formal materials, (c) is appropriate for letters and memos (d) a and b, (e) a and c.

10. ___ When adding headings, be sure to (a) use no more than two levels of headings, (b) make each higher-level heading yield at least three lower-level headings, (c) avoid using all capital letters, (d) include orphans periodically to show consistency (e) none of the above.

Additional Fill-In the Blank and Short Answer Questions

11. The definition of a sans-serif font is _____ and an example of this type of font is _____.

12. If you had a paragraph that you wanted to draw particular attention to, what are four different design strategies you might use to do so?

CHAPTER 9

Resumes and Other Employment Materials

This chapter marks a shift in the text from foundational skills to looking at particular genres of communication, applying the principles and strategies from previous chapters. From this point forward, each chapter concentrates on specific genres of writing.

Chapter 9 focuses on employment-related communications, including resumes, job application letters, interviews, thank you letters, and acceptance or refusal letters. The chapter stresses the importance of carefully evaluating one's own skills in relation to an employer's needs and the potential job. It provides suggestions for how to research potential employers to find an appropriate fit.

Using this information, applicants then need to tailor their communications so that they highlight key areas relevant to the particular employer of interest. A key element stressed throughout the chapter is the need to be specific and provide examples that support specific claims made about how the applicant's skills relate to the particular job.

In its discussion of developing resumes, the chapter addresses key parts to include (contact information, objective, key words, etc), potential organizing strategies, and essential formatting strategies for different methods of delivery including paper-based, online, scannable, and email delivery. It also indicates what not to include in these different delivery methods, advising that they be particularly cautious of divulging some personal information if the resume is posted online.

The letter-writing portion of the chapter addresses organizational and content strategies for solicited and unsolicited application letters that explain how the credentials fit the job and present an informed, professional, and likable persona.

After reading this chapter, students will be able to

- Know their skills and aptitudes and apply them to the job search process
- Narrow their job search and approach the job-search process
- Compose hard-copy and electronic resumes
- Compose a persuasive job applications letter
- Compile a dossier and a portfolio (or Webfolio)
- Be skilled at preparing for and going on job interviews
- Write an appropriate thank you letter
- Write an appropriate acceptance or refusal letter

TEACHING TIPS

Being gainfully employed is the one desire virtually all students have in common, so learning how to find and communicate with potential employers is one of the most critical skills they can learn in your course.

This point in the text is perhaps the most powerful "teachable moment" for reiterating the importance of audience considerations as the driving force in writing. Crafting job applications to the specific needs of the audience requires students to apply the concepts you've covered in the previous chapters such as integrating terminology that matters to the audience, choosing clear, direct, specific words, and emphasizing key information through organization and visual layout and design strategies.

Utilizing Career Center Resources

Virtually all campuses have career centers that produce an array of helpful career development workshops and materials. Unfortunately, most students never set foot in these centers. One way you can help students forge this link is to invite a representative to your class to provide a brief workshop. Or, you can at least distribute materials created by the center and provide Internet links to the center either in class or via a companion Web site to your class.

Emphasizing Transferrable Skills

Since students often have limited direct experiences with the jobs they might be applying for, one way to approach this gap is to encourage them to take advantage of internships and project work that will help them gain direct experience in their field. Another approach is to emphasize the concept of transferrable skills. Ask your class about what skills or qualities they think most employers might be looking for. Examples might include the following: taking initiative, working well in teams, being on-time, solving problems, and communicating effectively. Chapter 9 includes some of these transferrable skills in the "Assessing Your Skills and Aptitudes" section on page 158.

ADDITIONAL EXERCISES

1. **Defining Specific Applicable Experience.** Find a job opening that might appeal to you. Use a two-column sheet for this exercise. In the first column, in each row, identify each of the qualifications you believe the employer would want for that position. You will likely need to look outside of the job-posting description to fully understand the skills required (see "Researching the Job Market" in Chapter 9). In the second column, for each qualification, list specific experiences you have had indicating you have that skill. What evidence can you provide? This information provides a helpful blueprint for the key elements to emphasize in a resume tailored for that type of position.

   Caution: Be sure to watch for vague words or statements (*much, many, often,* etc). For example, instead of "worked with large teams" you might say "facilitated planning meetings involving 25 to 35 team members." This would indicate your role and specifics about how large the teams really were.

2. **Follow-Up Letter**. Evaluate the effectiveness of the follow-up letter below. How might it be improved? In a brief memo to your instructor, describe changes you would suggest.

Dear Melanie,

I really enjoyed meeting you and your staff last week. I had a great time and hope you and I will have a chance to work together in the near future. I look forward to talking with you soon.

Sincerely,

Mark Malou

3. **Keywords**. With the use of databases to store and search résumés, today's job environment requires applicants to incorporate key terms that potential employers may be looking for. In groups of three students with common areas of interest, choose a particular category of job in that field which might interest you. For example, students interested in marketing might work together to consider a copyrighting position and associated keywords.

Work together to develop a list of the top 15 keywords you think potential employers may be looking for. How might this impact your own approach toward résumé writing? What does this indicate about areas you might want to develop in your own experience background, and how might you gain that experience while being a student? Present your findings in class.

4. **Applying for Cross-Cultural Work.** In the current global economy, a great percentage of large companies operate in multiple countries. Imagine that you are applying for a job in your field that involves traveling to and working in another country periodically for projects. Other than the technical skills you might need for your job, what are other skills migh be necessary for you to demonstrate in your résumé to let your potential employer know that you are up for the challenges of working cross-culturally? Write a cover letter to a hypothetical employer, highlighting these skills and providing evidence from your experience.

80

CHAPTER 9 QUIZ

Indicate whether the statements 1 through 7 are TRUE or FALSE by writing T or F in the blank.

1. ___ To increase your employment chances, apply for the broadest possible jobs.

2. ___ Usually, readers scan a page quickly to get a sense of the overall readability of a document.

3. ___ The career-objective statement should be tailored to the specific job for which you are applying.

4. ___ To prepare a résumé for scanning, use asterisks instead of bullets.

5. ___ Starting with a question is too informal for a cover letter.

6. ___ During an employment interview, it is important to have your own set of questions to ask the potential employer, as they can be as important as the answers you give.

In items 7 through 10, choose the letter of the expression that best completes the statement.

7. ___ Most employers will look at a resume for (a) 3–5 minutes, (b) 2–3 minutes, (c) 1–2 minutes, (d) 15–45 seconds, (e) 5–15 seconds

8. ___ The major implied question posed by all employers is (a) why do you want to work here?, (b) what do you have to offer?, (c) where would you like to be in ten years?, (d) what are your long-term goals?, (e) what salary would you accept?

9. ___ Throughout your résumé, use (a) complete sentences, (b) abbreviations, (c) FULL CAPS, (d) passive constructions (e) action verbs.

10. ___ To create an effective online résumé (a) convert all action verbs to nouns, (b) include keywords as nouns, (c) include a home address, (d) a and b, (e) b and c.

11. What are three items you would NOT want to include in your Webfolio?

12. What are three ways in which scannable résumés are different than paper résumés that are not intended for scanning?

CHAPTER 10

Memos and Letters

This chapter covers two of the most common forms of communication in the workplace: memos and letters. For each type of communication, Chapter 10 discusses the most common uses and purposes, intended audiences, and appropriate formatting. In addition, it provides advice on achieving the right tone in these communications as well as when it is appropriate to use a direct versus an indirect approach to the subject matter.

After reading this chapter, students will be able to

- ∞   Identify the parts and format of a memo
- ∞   Achieve the right tone in a memo
- ∞   Determine when to take a direct or indirect approach in a memo
- ∞   Write an effective memo
- ∞   Identify the parts and formats of workplace letters
- ∞   Determine when to take a direct or indirect approach in a letter
- ∞   Write an effective inquiry, claim, sales, or adjustment letter

TEACHING TIPS

Next to Chapter 9, which emphasized employment-related documents, this chapter presents business documents that are most likely to be used by your students.

Addressing Email versus Memo

Nevertheless, students may not see the value of memos and letters at first, since so much of business communication seems to be via email today. Students may resist the whole discussion of memos, since many do not see the relevance in today's workplace. The way to address this is to point to the key fact that, as the chapter states, "emails themselves can function like memos." The basic parts of a memo, in fact, are built into the structure of emails (with the exception of the word "memo," of course!). As noted in Chapter 18 later in the text, the tone of emails used to be less formal. Because of their central role in today's workplace, the tone has become more formal, appropriate to that used with business colleagues.

Yet, the value of a paper memo is worth discussing. You might ask students to discuss the key benefits of using a paper version of a memo versus an electronic version. The chapter mentions, for example, how easy it is to miss an email in the midst of a stream of emails commonly received in a given workday. Paper actually stands out in the midst. The whole premise that "paper is dead" has been around for many years, yet we still seem to value hard copy for certain purposes. When should we be sending our messages electronically, and when should they be by paper? What underlying message is being sent by virtue of this decision alone? This question resurfaces in Chapter 18, which focuses specifically on digital communications.

Taking the "You" Perspective

The chapter's discussion of letters includes a detailed description of writing from the reader's perspective, not just the writer's perspective. Be sure to emphasize that this is an essential skill for all business communications, whether in letter format, email format, memo format, or any of the other formats they will be exploring. This is another way of addressing the attention to audience issues raised throughout the text.

ADDITIONAL EXERCISES

1. **New Business.** Your employer recently opened a dog daycare facility in a city that currently has 3 other such establishments. The other facilities are much larger than yours, with fancy features such as dog swimming pools and dog trainers on staff. Your facility can handle only 15 dogs at a time, but this provides you with opportunities for more personalized playtime with your

staff and smaller dog-group interactions to avoid overwhelming each dog with too much stimulus. Another key feature is your lower prices—while the community average price is $28 per day, you are able to charge just $20 per day because of your lower overhead costs. Like the other facilities, yours will also include a live Webcam so that the dog owners can watch their dogs play during the day. To encourage new customers, you will also offer a "buy 5 days, get one free" package discount.

As the office manager and publicity coordinator (remember, this is a small business), you have been asked to draft a sales letter announcing your business to a list of dog owners in the community. Be sure to apply the principles you learned about in Chapter 9, including an attention grabber, a description of the service, and a clear request that the readers take action.

2. **Memo Evaluation**. Working in pairs, evaluate the design and organizational structure of a memo from a workplace. This could be a memo currently used in one of your own companies or organizations, or one you obtain from someone else in the workplace. If it is a memo from your organization, be sure this is the type of memo you can share outside the company or that you have permission to do so with specific names crossed out.

To what degree does it include the basic parts and format indicated in your readings in Chapter 10?

- How appropriate is the tone?

- Does it take a direct or indirect approach, and was the choice appropriate?

- Overall, how effective is the memo? What changes might make it more effective?

- Does the memo fall within one of the basic types of memos presented in the chapter, or is it another type of memo?

Complete your evaluation in a 1–2 page memo to your instructor.

3. **Dropping a Customer**. You are the manager of a health club that is 10 years old. One of your first customers was Bob Blue, a well-connected businessman in town who has been coming to your club faithfully for the

85

past decade. Unfortunately, during that time, he has also become increasingly rude to your staff. In the past year, he has belligerently demanded extra towels, extra time on the courts, and entrance without showing his membership card because of his status as being the longest-running customer. When the staff has tried to enforce the same rules on Mr. Blue as those applied to other members, Mr. Blue has cursed loudly and stomped through the club, making other members and the staff very uncomfortable. You have personally talked with Mr. Blue on three occasions, asking that he respect the club's rules. Nevertheless, the behavior has continued. You have decided to write Mr. Blue a letter, temporarily suspending his membership for a period of six months, at which point a renewed membership may be considered with a waiver of the joiner's fee. Write a letter to Mr. Blue, informing Mr. Blue of your decision while also attempting to avoid a rift that might cause Mr. Blue to use his extensive network of contacts to bring your club down.

4. **Gleaning Further Guidance.** Probably one of the most common forms of letters is the complaint letter. Work in groups of 3–4. As a supplement to the materials presented in your text, research advice on strategies for writing good complaint letters. Of your findings, what are the top five strategies you would add to the strategies you learned about in the text? Which of these strategies might be the most difficult to apply? Why? How might you work through those difficulties?

CHAPTER 10 QUIZ.

Indicate whether the statements 1 through 7 are TRUE or FALSE by writing T or F in the blank.

1. ___ The most typical form of everyday workplace communication is a letter.

2. ___ Headings and bullets are not needed in memos because they are typically short communications.

3. ___ An email "signature" is not legally binding.

4. ___ Memos generally focus on only one topic.

5. ___ Letters are preferred for communicating outside an organization.

6. ___ In a letter, the date always appears immediately below the sender's address.

7. ___ Organizing questions in a numbered list can increase your chances of a response in an inquiry letter.

In items 8 through 10, choose the letter of the expression that best completes the statement.

8. ___ Memos (a) are commonly addressed to people outside a company, (b) provide appropriate formality for the workplace, (c) should always take a direct approach, (d) should be sent via paper rather than email, (e) none of the above.

9. ___ A transmittal memo (a) distributes bad news to the recipients (b) distributes good news to the recipients, (c) accompanies long reports or proposals, (d) a and b, (e) c and d

10. ___ In a letter of complaint (a) an indirect approach is appropriate for arguable claims, (b) an indirect approach is appropriate for routine claims, (c) a direct approach is always the most effective, (d) a direct approach is appropriate for arguable claims, (e) an indirect approach is always appropriate.

Additional Fill-In the Blank and Short Answer Questions

11. Adjustment letters are written in response to _____.

12. When would you want to use an indirect approach?

CHAPTER 11

Definitions

This chapter addresses how to make specialized terms and concepts accessible to people who may not have expertise in the field.

As with all elements of technical communication, attention to the audience is crucial here. Knowing what the audience needs to know involves evaluating what the audience currently knows about the term or concept and related terms or concepts. It is also critical to know why the audience needs to know about it— what context will the audience be using the term in and for what purpose? The answers to these questions, and how well definitions address them, have a range of legal, ethical, and social implications.

Definitions fall into three distinct categories: parenthetical, sentence, and expanded definitions. The level of detail will depend upon the needs of the audience, and many documents will contain a combination of these three types of definitions.

- **Parenthetical Definitions**—clarifies the meaning of a word by simply using a more familiar synonym or a clarifying phrase in parenthesis immediately after the word.

- **Sentence Definitions**—states the term, then the broader class to which this item belongs, followed by the features that distinguish it from other items in that general grouping.

- **Expanded Definitions**—in a paragraph to several pages, provides a much more detailed definition using one or more methods of expansion such as exploring the word's origin (etymology), explaining what the term does not mean, comparing it to other terms, using visuals, and a range of other strategies discussed in the chapter.

89

The chapter concludes by discussing various ways to place definitions in relation to the main document. A short definition might be placed within a paragraph in parenthesis, for example, or in a marginal note. Expanded definitions are usually appropriate at the beginning of a document or as part of an appendix. Hyperlinks are another option to quickly and easily link the reader to key definitions while helping them to easily return to their original place in the document.

After reading this chapter, students will be able to

- Appreciate the role of definition in clear and precise communication

- Consider audience and purpose when writing definitions

- Understand the legal, ethical, and societal implications of definitions

- Identify the three types of definitions

- Utilize various methods to expand a definition, as the situation requires

- Place definitions in their documents for greatest effectiveness

TEACHING TIPS

Corporate Culture and Definitions

The issue of terminology and definitions can open up an interesting dialogue with students about different corporate cultures, or even subcultures within a corporation, and the power of definition to separate or link workers across the workforce, even within a particular discipline. Different groups use different terms for the same item—for example "router" versus "tracking form." What implications might this have for training people across all teams? How might a company address the issue of different subcultures (IT versus marketing) using different terminology? One approach might be to create a corporate terminology for use by everyone. Another might be a shared corporate glossary that incorporates the terminology of each unit.

Keeping Track of Terminology Changes

An important point to emphasize here is the need to stay current with the terminology being used in one's chosen field as well as the broader culture. This is critical for not only understanding what others are saying, but also for maintaining credibility. Using older terminology can imply that a person's skills, too, are outdated. You might relate this to your discussion of the Chapter 9 materials regarding creating resumes and other employment-related documents. How does a person stay current? This is a rich source of discussion for your students to consider.

ADDITIONAL EXERCISES

1. **Exercises in Creating Sentence Definitions.** For each of the following terms, create sentence definitions. Assume that your audience is a member of the general public with a basic high school science background who is reading this term in a public education pamphlet. After each definition, cite at least four sources that you referred to in creating your definition.

    - **limnology**

    - **bioremediation**

    - **wetland**

    - **calcification**

    - **osteoporosis**

2. **Internal Hyperlinking.** Find a paper that you recently wrote for a course. Identify three terms that you should have defined. Write definitions for each. Create a glossary for the end of the document and use the internal bookmarking and hyperlinking features of your word processing software to create links to those definitions in your newly created glossary.

3. **Wikipedia Definitions.** When looking for the meaning of terms, writers often look toward Wikepedia as a source of definitions. In groups of 3 with students interested in common field, use Wikipedia to find the definition of a term from your field.

91

- Which strategies for defining are applied in the Wikipedia definition?

- How accurate does the definition seem to you?

- How does it compare to the definitions provided by at least two other sources that you find?

- How reliable do you think Wikipedia is as a source of definitions in your field?

Present your analysis to class in a brief presentation.

CHAPTER 11 QUIZ

Indicate whether the statements 1 through 7 are TRUE or FALSE by writing T or F in the blank.

1. ___ Parenthetical definitions are often synonyms.

2. ___ Definitions can be as long as several pages.

3. ___ Definitions can have legal implications.

4. ___ Hyperlinked definitions are difficult for readers to use.

5. ___ Circular definitions help clarify technical concepts.

6. ___ Visuals are inappropriate methods for defining concepts.

7. ___Use sentence definitions to establish a working definition of a term.

In items 8 through 10, choose the letter of the expression that best completes the statement.

8. ___ The specific strategies of expansion you choose will depend on (a), the needs of your audience (b) how much time you have, (c) the information you have, (d) the amount of space you have in your report, (e) none of these.

9. ___Definitions should be (a) judgmental (b) engaging, (c) impressionistic, (d) eclectic, (e) concise.

10. ___An expanded definition should be placed (a) at the beginning of a long document, (b) in an appendix, (c) as part of the running text, (d) a or b, depending upon the purpose, (e) none of these.

Additional Fill-In the Blank and Short Answer Questions

11. List the three parts of a sentence definition.

12. Besides etymology, history, and background, list three strategies for expanding definitions.

94

CHAPTER 12

Descriptions

In contrast to definitions (see Chapter 11), which explain the meaning of words and concepts, descriptions are depictions of physical products and processes that help readers visualize what they look like and how they work. Descriptions are vitally important in workplace writing because, like definitions, they ensure that readers understand the full meaning of any technical document.

Descriptions generally fall into two categories: product and process descriptions. Product descriptions help users understand the parts of an item, and process descriptions help users understand the steps or stages in an event.

Whichever type of description, the writer needs to be sure it meets the specific needs of the intended audience and the purpose of the description to the audience. The description should then use the following strategies:

- Maintain objectivity

- Be concise, supplying only what the audience needs

- Include the necessary parts: a clear and limiting title, an orienting introduction, the appropriate sequence of topics (spatial, functional, chronological—or a combination), and a conclusion that brings readers full circle.

- Incorporate visuals that enhance the verbal description

The chapter concludes by addressing a particular type of description—the specification. This indicates what is to be done and it is to be done according to a set of standards. Specifications are important for maintaining consistency, quality, and safety.

After reading this chapter, students will be able to

- Understand the importance of descriptions in workplace communication

- Maintain objectivity in descriptions

- Differentiate between product descriptions and process descriptions

- Write a long set of product or process descriptions

- Differentiate product or process descriptions from specifications

- Compose a set of specifications

TEACHING TIPS

On the job, many students will write descriptions of products and mechanisms, and they should be aware that such descriptions demand format and depth of detail that go beyond the requirements of the ordinary descriptive essay they are used to writing in school and that such descriptions must be impartial and precise. In contrast, the structure of the essay (by definition a personal form) elicits descriptions from an expressive rather than a technical point of view.

Writing descriptions may sound quite straightforward to students, who might mistakenly believe that impartial means that all descriptions will sound essentially the same. We don't describe simply for the sake of describing. Our subject, our intention, and what we know of our readers' needs dictate our direction and the amount of detail we include. As with other aspects of technical writing, remind students that creating effective descriptions requires making informed choices.

Introducing Descriptions Through an In-Class Exercise

Most students (especially lower levels) initially have trouble generating finite descriptive details. One good classroom exercise for overcoming this problem is a variation of brainstorming. Bring to class some mundane and somewhat complex items, such as a coleus plant or a staple remover or a paper punch. Place the item on a table at the front of the class with a ruler positioned conspicuously nearby. Ask the class to write a short piece, on the spot, describing the item or mechanism to someone who has never seen such a thing.

After much sweating and grumbling, most students will produce a short piece that is somewhat disorganized and so general as to be meaningless—except for one or two vivid details. Now ask the class as a group to begin assigning descriptive details to the item.

Sooner or later, one of them will think to pick up the ruler and measure specific parts. As the details appear, write them all out on the board. Record everything—even those subjective descriptions such as "pretty" and "ugly." Within ten minutes, you should have enough material to fill your chalkboard.

Next, ask the class to weed out the subjective from the objective. Next, ask them to classify the objective details by dividing the assortment into groups, according to shared characteristics (for the plant: leaves, stem, potting soil, pot; for the staple remover: prongs, plastic finger grips, spring mechanism). Finally, arrange the various classes of detail in the most logical sequence for description (for the plant: from bottom to top, or vice versa; for the staple remover, from finger grips to plastic exterior to hollow metal prongs, including pointed tips and arms, to the coil-spring extensor mechanism). Now decide as a group on the intended audience: Who is it? Why does he or she need the information (to be able to recognize the plant; to manufacture the staple remover, to understand its function)?

After completing this exercise, students should understand what you mean by descriptive details; they should know how to classify data, how to choose the best descriptive sequence, and how to select the appropriate details to fill the reader's specific needs.

ADDITIONAL EXERCISES

1. **Evaluating a Description.** Using the company Web site evaluate a description of a product. Write a 1–2 page analysis of the description considering the following aspects:

   - Who do you think the intended audience is for this description?

   - Is there a clear and limiting title? If not, what alternative title would you suggest?

   - Is there an introduction that tells the reader what to look for? If not, write a one-sentence introduction.

- Which type of sequencing did the authors use in the description?

- How effectively were visuals used to explain the product?

- How effective was the conclusion?

2. **Limiting the Scope of Descriptions**. As a communicator, one of your key decisions is to know what not to include, as well as what to include. While this is an important consideration in virtually all forms of technical communication, consider how this applies when writing descriptions.

In groups of four, discuss what information you might want to be sure to leave out in a description of a new organic air freshener. The intended audience is potential home users of the product. Write a list of key aspects you would exclude for this audience but which might serve a descriptive purpose. Once you have the list of exclusions, brainstorm which audiences you think would be interested in knowing these items in a description and for what purposes. Compare your ideas with those of another group. Where do you agree or disagree?

3. **Visual Depictions of Processes**. Using the Web, use the advanced search features of a search engine to specifically search for images of processes. Browse through the different types of images you find, looking first at the images by themselves, but then looking at where they appear in their original online documents.

- Which three images have you found seem to be particularly effective in describing a process?

- What aspects of the images are particularly powerful?

- How do they focus the reader's attention on the important details of the process?

- How well do the images work with the accompanying information about the processes?

- How might you apply one or more of the visual strategies you found to depict a process with which you are familiar? Sketch out a visual design of that process using the successful features you gleaned from the examples you found.

Present your images and analysis to your classmates in a brief oral presentation.

CHAPTER 12 QUIZ

Indicate whether the statements 1 through 7 are TRUE or FALSE by writing T or F in the blank.

1. ___ The main purpose of all technical descriptions is to stimulate consumer interest in products.

2. ___ Except for promotional writing, descriptions should be objective.

3. ___ Ethical communicators do not express personal opinions, even when a product may be unsafe or unsound.

4. ___ Users of any technical description need as much information as possible.

5. ___ Any item can be described in many ways.

6. ___ Customers are the primary audience for specifications.

7. ___ Use prose sparingly when writing specifications—prefer short lists instead.

8. ___ Specifications are a type of description.

In items 9 and 10, choose the letter of the expression that best completes the statement.

9. ___ The most precise technical descriptions are (a), creative (b) vividly subjective, (c) visionary, (d) objective, (e) all of these.

10. ___ When creating specifications to meet your audience (a) always avoid specialized industry language, (b) you can use specialized language when your audience is primarily technical experts, (c) avoid referring to outside sources of information for more details, (d) a and c, (e) none of these.

Additional Fill-In the Blank and Short Answer Questions

11. If a description includes a title, introduction, and a sequence of topics, what two additional elements are missing from the description?

12. Besides spatial sequence, list two possible sequences for describing an item.

101

CHAPTER 13

Instructions and Procedures

This chapter addresses instructions, which lay out steps for completing a task or a series of tasks. Procedures are a type of instructions that provide official guidelines for people who are familiar with a task, ensuring that all members of a group coordinate their activities when performing a task. When writing these types of documents, it is important to consider the ethical and legal implications, keeping user safety at the forefront. To ensure that instructions and procedures will, indeed, be effective, a writer should conduct a usability analysis to test their accuracy and ease of use.

Instructions

The most common formats for instructions are instructional brochures, user manuals, quick-reference cards, hyperlinked instructions, and computer instructions. Whichever format, instructions should include:

- a title that provides a clear, exact preview of the task or tasks

- a brief overview or introduction that explains the purpose of the instructions and what they contain

- a body section with the required steps, each step in numbered order and sub-steps beginning on a new line

In addition, instructions might include a range of other components such as a conclusion to summarize the tasks, expected results, or troubleshooting tips; helpful visuals to accompany the text; notes to add essential information; cautions, warnings, and/or danger notices.

Instructions should be written at the level of detail and technicality appropriate for the intended audience. They should also be clear and easy to follow, applying principles of effective design and style suggested in the chapter.

Procedures

Unlike other types of instructions, which will be read mostly by users unfamiliar with the given task, procedures may be used by people already familiar with a procedure but who need to follow a standard. The most common types of procedures are standard operating procedures (SOPs), general safety procedures, and medical or health procedures.

After reading this chapter, students will be able to

- Identify the various types of instructions and how they are used

- Understand the ethical and legal implications of instructions

- Understand the components of instructions

- Determine the level of detail and technicality necessary for a given set of instructions

- Write instructions with a readable style and accessible design

- Understand the components of procedures

- Write a set of procedures

- Test instructions and procedures for usability

TEACHING TIPS

At first, students often feel that writing instructions is a simple task. By having students evaluate examples of instructions and write instructions of their own, they will realize that well-written instructions require careful attention to audience and context of use, clear writing, and effective design. In short, instructions are as complicated, if not more, to create as other aspects of technical writing they will encounter.

Developing an Appreciation for Clarity—In-Class Exercise

To help students develop audience awareness and awareness of other key issues of creating instructions, try the following simple in-class exercise:

Bring to class a loaf of bread and a jar of jelly so that students can do a hands-on user test of this instructions exercise. (We've avoided peanut putter in this exercise because of common food allergies.) Ask each student to take ten to fifteen minutes to write instructions for making a peanut butter and jelly sandwich. Assume the reader knows what jelly, peanut butter, knife, and bread are, but the reader has arrived from a country that does not have screw-cap jars, plastic bags, or sandwiches. You can expect several students to be skeptical about this exercise, but be persistent. Ask them to develop instructions that give the reader all of the information needed to complete the task successfully. Ask for five student volunteers to present their instructions, and five student volunteers to be testers. Run through each set of instructions in front of class with the matched writer/tester pair. The class will notice a range of issues, often related to using language imprecisely or making too many assumptions about a reader's background and ability to fill in information gaps. This exercise then becomes a jumping off point for the need to carefully analyze audience background and clearly present the steps needed. It also drives home the important role of user testing in the writing and revision stages, harkening back to Chapter 2's emphasis on user testing as well as the user-testing material in Chapter 13.

Integrating Group Work into Instructions

As you consider what types of assignments or in-class exercises to incorporate for this topic, you might make creating instructions a core group-written assignment for your course. Students can work through assigning various roles and tasks related to this assignment, including audience analysis, developing the visuals, integrating them into the document, describing each step, ensuring that the overall design and style meet the needs of the intended audience, designing and delivering user-tests, and revising, and providing a group analysis of the process.

In developing a draft, testing the instructions, making revisions, and reflecting on the group, the group will need to work through key communication issues to be successful. You might provide in-class time for this, but it is also important that students learn how to negotiate asynchronous communications for drafting documents as well to be prepared for the modern workplace. You might ask the students to submit a group process workbook that documents all group communications along the way—summaries of key meetings, copies of emails or classroom discussion board postings, etc.

ADDITIONAL EXERCISES

1. **Group-Written Instructions**. In groups of 3–5, create a set of instructions for the assembly of an item that has at least 15 different pieces to assemble. The assembled object can be something that actually exists (such as an instrument or household item), or it can be something you make up (such as an assembly of Legos or other items into an object your group decides on a name and purpose for). You may want to review the materials on writing in groups covered in Chapter 2 of the text before beginning this project.

   First, analyze the audience who will be using the instructions. Then, create the main sections of instructions indicated in Chapter 13 and any additional sections needed. Make sure you apply the Strategies for Creating an Effective Design and the Strategies for Achieving Readability noted in the chapter as well. User-test your instructions on at least three different people. Using their feedback, make revisions to your instructions.

   Write a group-written memo to your instructor that

   - Describes the audience for your instructions

   - Discusses changes you made to your instructions based on user feedback

   - Note the main contributions of each person on your writing team

   - Take-away lessons you learned from the process of creating these instructions that you might apply in future writing projects

   Attach the instructions and include your unassembled pieces so that your instructor can also try out the instructions you have created.

106

2. **Revision Exercise**. Evaluate and revise the following set of instructions:

Making a Bed

A person should take the bottom sheet and tuck it over each corner of the mattress. Once the bottom sheet has been secured, the top sheet should be spread across the bottom sheet so that it covers the whole bed. The bottom and sides of the top sheet should be tucked in. As you are tucking the sheet in, be sure to avoid bending your fingernails back due to the wait of the mattress over your hand as you slide the bottom of the sheet under to tuck it. The top of the sheet should be folded back so that it looks presentable. Each pillow should be slid into a pillowcase that matches the sheets. Caution: The side of the pillow with the tag hanging off should go into the pillowcase first so that it doesn't stick out of the pillowcase and scratch the sleeper. Once you have the pillows in their cases, place them at the top of the bed. Lastly, place the cover on top of the bed, covering the sheets. Fold back the cover so that the pillows are visible.

3. **Video Instructions.** It used to be quite expensive to create instructional videos and distribute them, but with the advent of low-cost video cameras, video software, and free video-hosting services such as YouTube, these type of instructions are becoming much more common. Use the Web to find a video instruction for a product or procedure. To what extent does the video incorporate the principles you learned about in this chapter? What are specific advantages of delivering instructions using this format? What are potential disadvantages? How might the instructional video be improved to meet the intended audience and purpose of the video?

CHAPTER 13 QUIZ.

Indicate whether the statements 1 through 8 are TRUE or FALSE by writing T or F in the blank.

1. ___To avoid cluttering your instructions, use as few transitional phrases as possible.

2. ___Be careful to avoid redundancies between the visual and verbal information in instructions.

3. ___ The audience for procedures is typically people who are already familiar with the task.

4. ___ A usability study is appropriate for instructions but not procedures.

5. ___ Any item can be described in many ways.

6. ___Customers are the primary audience for specifications.

7. ___Use prose sparingly when writing specifications—short lists are preferred instead.

8. ___ Specifications are a type of description.

   In items 9 and 10, choose the letter of the expression that best completes the statement.

9. ___ When choosing the phrasing of each step of the instructions, use (a) parallel phrasing, (b) imperative mood, (c) active voice, (d) affirmative phrasing, (e) all of these.

10. ___Any visual in a set of instructions should be (a) placed in an appendix so as no to interrupt the steps, (b) placed in the introduction to increase interest, (c) incorporated within the discussion of the related step, for immediate reference, (d) a or b, (e) a or c.

Additional Fill-In the Blank and Short Answer Questions

11. In addition to having a body, both instructions and procedures must include a _____.

12. What are the three most common types of procedures?

CHAPTER 14

Summaries

In today's rapid-pace workplace, summaries play a critical role in helping readers glean the main ideas and essential information contained in longer documents. By providing information in a compressed, less technical form, summaries help readers decide whether to read the full document, or specific parts of it, and they provide a framework for understanding the full document if they do choose to read it.

This chapter emphasizes four main aspects of effective summaries: accuracy, completeness, conciseness, and nontechnical style. Students learn a step-by-step process for creating effective summaries by

- carefully reading the original document,

- re-reading and marking the essential material, cutting and pasting essential material,

- redrafting and reorganizing the information,

- editing the draft for conciseness, clarity, and grammatical correctness, and

- comparing the summary to the original draft to make sure the summary stays true to the original meaning, intent, or emphasis of the original.

In addition to describing the process of summarizing other writer's works, the chapter addresses four main types of internal summaries that the original author might create: closing summaries, informative abstracts, descriptive abstracts, and executive summaries. Regardless of the kind of summary, it's important that writers try to avoid ethical pitfalls such as distorting the original message through choices about what to leave in and out and what to emphasize.

After reading this chapter, students will be able to

- Summarize a long document using the step-by-step strategies

- Identify the purpose and placement of the four types of summaries: closing summaries, informative abstracts, descriptive abstracts, and executive summaries

- Recognize the ethical issues when writing summaries

TEACHING TIPS

Using Summaries as a Building Block for Other Work

Summaries are a logical early assignment because they

- apply the principles of audience analysis and clear prose writing in specific practices

- provide a means for writing efficiently and concisely

- improve note-taking and study skills in other courses by helping students recognize and differentiate major from minor points

- provide practice in writing informative paragraphs that are unified and coherent

- teach students to extract the essential message from a longer piece and to communicate it intact, helping to develop a skill they will use throughout the semester

Common Points of Confusion

One of the most common errors made by students in papers is to introduce new material in a summary because they think it might interest a reader. However, an important point to reiterate here is that nothing should be introduced in a summary that wasn't indicated in the original document. This is a nuance often missed.

When creating summaries for their own work rather than someone else's, many students try to write their summary before their full content is completed. Remind students that summaries are based on an original document that must be completed first.

ADDITIONAL EXERCISES

1. **Executive Summary Analysis.** Grant proposals rely on executive summaries to engage the reader and provide a complete summary that motivates potential donors to say "yes" to the proposal. Locate a grant proposal that includes an executive summary. Evaluate the executive summary according to the Checklist for Summaries in Chapter 13. What, if anything, would need to be changed to make the summary more effective?

2. **Summary Comparisons.** Find a research paper you have written in a previous course and create an informative abstract of no more than 150 words and a descriptive abstract of no more than 350 words. The audience for the summaries is college students wanting to look up papers on these issues for their own research. Next, exchange your original paper (without the abstracts you've created) with another student in your class and create an informative and descriptive abstract of your classmate's paper. Once you both have your abstracts completed, share the summaries with each other.
    *   How do your summaries of the same work compare?
    *   Did your peer's summary of your work seem like a true summary? Was anything left out you felt was important to include? Was more emphasis given to particular points than you intended?
    *   What assumptions did you and your classmate make about what was essential vs. non-essential?

3. **Group-Written Summaries.** Use a collaborative writing tool such as Googledocs or a wiki to complete this assignment. As a group, write a summary of an article you agree on for an audience you define. The summary should be no more than 400 words. As a group, present your process of writing the summary in class. How did you decide on what to include or exclude? Where is there agreement or disagreement about what to include or exclude? What organizational strategy did you decide on? What was considered but dropped?

4. **Audience Considerations**. Your local public health department has decided to focus its efforts towards encouraging people to eat more nuts because of the potential health benefits. The campaign plans to focus its education efforts towards three main audiences: people over 55, children, and college students. As part of the campaign, they need a two-sentence summary of the primary health benefits.

Using the Web, find three articles on the health benefits of eating nuts (or a particular nut). Create the following versions of your summary:

- a summary that would be appropriate for all of the audiences

- a summary that would be particularly appropriate for seniors

- a summary that would be particularly appropriate for children

- a summary that might be particularly appropriate for college students

What changes did you make to your summaries to accommodate for each of these audiences, and why? What assumptions about your audiences helped you decide what to include or exclude?

Write a memo directed to the Outreach Team of the Public Health Department that includes each of your summaries and justifies your choices. Also include complete reference information for each of the three articles you used to create your summary.

CHAPTER 14 QUIZ.

Indicate whether the statements 1 through 8 are TRUE or FALSE by writing T or F in the blank.

1. ____ Summaries use a nontechnical style.

2. ____ Writing summaries requires distinguishing between essential and superfluous details.

3. ____ Summaries are an opportunity for the writer to put his or her own emphasis on particular aspects of the original material.

4. ____ Informative abstracts are one- or two-sentence descriptions of what a document contains.

5. ____ Closing summaries appear just after the "Recommendations" section of a report.

6. ____ Formal reports always include informative abstracts or executive summaries.

7. ____ Executive summaries are more persuasive than descriptive summaries.

8. ____ A summary should include additional details and examples not found in the original document but which support the main points of the original.

In items 9 and 10, choose the letter of the expression that best completes the statement.

9. ____ Effective summaries (a) use the same wording as the original, (b) let readers know what to expect in the full document, (c) follow the same logical sequence as the original, (d) a and c, (e) all of these.

10. ____ Descriptive abstracts (a) are more extensive than informative abstracts, (b) appear right after the table of contents in a report, (c) describe in detail what the document contains, (d) are usually 3–5 paragraphs long, (e) help people decide whether to read the entire report.

Additional Fill-In the Blank and Short Answer Questions

11. List the four types of internal summaries.

12. List the four key characteristics of effective summaries.

116

CHAPTER 15

Informal Reports

This chapter's focus is on the most commonly written reports in the workplace, short reports that serve either an informational or analytical functions. Whereas the primary purpose of information reports is to inform an audience, the purpose of analytical reports is to offer both information and conclusions based on the information. The chapter provides strategies and examples of four types of information reports (progress reports, periodic activity reports, trip reports, and meeting minutes) and three types of analytical reports (feasibility reports, recommendation reports, and peer review reports).

After reading this chapter, students will be able to

- Define and understand the importance of informal reports

- Identify the difference between informational and analytical reports

- Plan and write effective informational reports

- Plan and write effective analytical reports

TEACHING TIPS

The shorter analytical and recommendation reports in this chapter provide helpful background to the following chapter, which focuses on longer, more in-depth and formal analytical reports. One potential strategy you might consider taking is to have students initially develop a shorter recommendation report, but then have them expand their analysis into a more formal report later in the course.

Many of the information reports covered in this chapter—progress reports, peer review reports, and meeting minutes—are helpful to incorporate into longer projects your students may work on during over several weeks. By assigning them as part of larger projects, you can also help reinforce the fact that these types of reports are usually part of an ongoing relationship among colleagues.

Assigning Progress Reports as Interim Deliverables in Longer Projects

Most technical writing courses include a longer, formal report or proposal that students work on over several weeks. One inevitable fact of virtually all projects is that they rarely go as planned: research strategies sometimes fall through and need to be adjusted (e.g. too few surveys pan out), or the scope turns out to be broad and needs to be narrowed. This is a point you may want to acknowledge up front when you assign these longer projects. Progress reports are important not just for reporting what has been done and will be done, but also to help the reader accept changes along the way. So, though they are primarily informational documents, they are also persuasive. Progress reports need to persuade the reader that to trust that the project will, indeed, be completed and, if needed, they need to persuade the reader to accept proposed changes to the original plan.

Integrating the Peer Review Report into a Group Project

Learning to provide honest, respectful, and tactful feedback to peers is a critical skill in today's workplace where periodic reviews of colleagues is commonplace. Since most courses involve an ongoing group project, you might consider integrating a peer review report into the group project process. Each team member in a group project could review the performance and participation of other team members thus far, providing constructive criticism addressed to each team member. This allows for some mid-course correction in team dynamics. As is often the case in the workplace, you might have this be anonymous feedback to fellow student. You would then also have this feedback submitted to you as well for credit.

ADDITIONAL EXERCISES

1. **Minutes and the Eye of the Beholder.** Working in groups of 3 to 4, attend a meeting or view the same meeting as a streamed archive online (many city council meetings are available as online video streams).

    Step 1. Individually prepare minutes. Each team member should create his or her own set of minutes based on individual observations and notes. Be sure to apply the textbook's strategies for effective meeting minutes.

Step 2. Compare versions of minutes. After completing each set of minutes, view each other's versions and compare the similarities and differences. What differences do you notice about what was left in or out of the minutes? What organizational tools and other design strategies seem most effective?

Step 3. Redraft the minutes as one unified version and report on decisions made. Create a final version of the minutes. Select one person from the group to report back to the class on what you learned as a group about the process and product of writing minutes.

2. **Creating a Template for a Periodic Report**. Work in groups of 4 for this exercise.

   Review Examples: Find examples on the Web or examples from your workplace to find different types of periodic activity reports. How are these documents structured to help the readers quickly determine whether projects are on track? How do the page layout, font choices, and font formatting (including color) serve the purposes of these communications? What visuals strategies seemed most effective?

   Create a Template: Drawing from the samples you reviewed, create a periodic report design with placeholders for main sections of a periodic report that could be used in a sports store that must report to its parent company on a monthly basis. Consider what items might need to be tracked and develop a report structure for this information. Corporate headquarters will want this template to be used by all 50 stores in the chain.

3. **Feasibility Report**. A local coffee shop in your town, Buzzed, decides that it wants to try to help meet the needs of customers who are intolerant to gluten. The owner, Heather Haloo, has asked you to research the feasibility of offering some gluten-free baked goods for these customers. Currently, there is no baking facility at the coffee shop; all baked goods are contracted through other vendors. Research the feasibility of this gluten-free addition change in offerings, and write a feasibility report directed to Heather Haloo. Be sure to follow the Strategies for Feasibility Reports in Chapter 15.

CHAPTER 15 QUIZ

Indicate whether the statements 1 through 7 are TRUE or FALSE by writing T or F in the blank.

1. ____ Most informal reports are formatted as a memorandum.

2. ____ Periodic activity reports and progress reports are the same—they are two names for the same type of report.

3. ____ Progress reports for external clients should be delivered via email.

4. ____ A peer review report is a type of recommendation report.

5. ____ Peer review reports should avoid suggesting alternative courses of action when providing constructive criticism, as this is too presumptive and does not allow the peer to investigate potential solutions to the issues raised.

6. ____ Minutes serve as an official record of a meeting.

7. ____ Minutes are often distributed via email.

In items 8 through 10, choose the letter of the expression that best completes the statement.

8. ____ Analytical reports (a) provide information, (b) provide conclusions, (c) evaluate and interpret information, (d) a and b, (e) a, b, and c.

9. ____ Trip reports should (a) avoid cluttering the document with the details of who was spoken with and where, since the focus is on the financial details of the trip, (b) avoid expressing personal impressions, (c) express a willingness to answer follow-up questions, (d) b and c, (e) a, b, and c.

10. ____ Feasibility reports and recommendation reports are similar in that they both (a) have managers and other decision makers as their primary audience, (b) emphasize expected rather than possible benefits, (c) discuss the problem or situation before the recommendation, (d) a and b, (e) all of the above.

11. List four different types of informational reports.

12. A clear title of meeting minutes should include what two elements?

CHAPTER 16

Formal Reports

Formal reports are more professional and longer than informal reports discussed in Chapter 15. The formal report format replaces the informal memo format when the topic requires lengthy discussion. Distinguishing them from informal reports, formal reports generally include a title page, a table of contents, a system of headings, a list of references or works cited, and other front-matter and end-matter supplements.

Formal reports generally take one of three different approaches, each answering a different key question:

1. **the comparative approach**, which rates similar items on the basis of specific criteria (the report will answer: "Which is better, X or Y?"),
2. **the causal approach**, which explains the immediate and distant causes of something (the report will answer: "Why does X occur?"),
3. **the feasibility approach**, which assesses the practicality of an idea or plan (the report will answer: "Is X a good idea?").

The chapter reiterates the importance of applying strategies that were alluded to earlier in the text. Formal reports should include accurate, appropriate, and interpreted data; a clearly identified purpose statement; an understandable structure; a readable style; audience-centered visuals; and a user-friendly design.

After reading this chapter, students will be able to

- Differentiate between informal and formal reports

- Determine the audience and purpose of formal reports

- Identify the characteristics of the three analytical approaches: comparative, causal, and feasibility

- Write a formal report that incorporates all the vital elements

- Include all of the essential parts in a formal report (front matter, text features, and end matter)

TEACHING TIPS

Weaving Formal Reports Throughout Your Course

Formal reports are where all of the pieces of the puzzle are integrated—to accomplish this successfully, students will need to apply the research, analysis, writing, and design skills they have learned throughout your course. Students should select their topics early in the semester and ideally apply many of their earlier assignments (e.g. memo, research, summary, proposal, progress reports) to move closer toward this final report. Early in your course, go over several analytical report samples, including the example in Chapter 16, in order that students have a sense of the final goal with this type of project.

Encourage students to choose practical topics they can use in their own workplace or organizations with which they are involved; this will keep them more interested and engaged. This type of assignment also lends itself well to primary research, which students often have minimal experience with from previous courses, despite its emphasis in the workplace.

Integrating Data into Reports

Emphasize that dropping raw data into the reader's lap is not enough. Evaluation and interpretation of data are crucial to the reader's understanding. A clear way to get this across to students is to remind them that a reader will pose a key question that they will need to answer for the reader: How does this data relate to something I care about? Once again, the approach to analyzing and interpreting data requires a careful audience and purpose analysis.

Addressing Front and End Matter

Save front and end matter sections until students are well along in planning, researching, and writing a draft of their report. As you cover the use of references, refer students to Appendix B for how to address documentation. Unless you have a preference, ask them to select a documentation system.

Applying Effective Design Strategies

Students might need to be reminded that it is OK to be creative with visual design to engage the readers. Look at multiple documents in class and discuss with students the different visual design strategies they notice. By reviewing these formal, longer documents, they will likely notice a range of visual devices that can serve as inspiration for their own report design. You might, for example, notice pullout quotes, boxes to frame key concepts, in-column notations, different uses of color to segment the document, font formatting strategies, etc.

ADDITIONAL EXERCISES

1. **Automating Table of Contents Creation.** Creating professional-looking outlines is easy if you use the features built into your word processing software. The style feature of your software allows it to quickly ascertain the main sections of your document and quickly generate a visually engaging table of contents. Using either an outline of your current analytical report or the full draft, first format the main headings using the style feature of your word processing program. Then, use the table of contents feature to generate your table of contents for the document. Try out a few different formatting options that might be available. Submit your outline or draft, along with a table of contents.

2. **Referencing and Citing.** Using Appendix A in the textbook, choose one of the citation styles to use (e.g. MLA, APA). For each source, write a sentence that would need to refer to that source—include the appropriate information in the sentence according to the citation style you have chosen. Then, create a reference list that includes all three references, formatted according to your chosen citation style.

3. **Formal-Report Case Study.** As the procurement manager for a roofing company, you have been asked by your supervisor to recommend a cell phone provider that offers services in your state. Your company takes jobs in both rural and urban areas, and it is important for safety reasons as well as other business reasons that the phone has reliable service. In addition to talking on the phone, employees will also need to send brief text messages to and from headquarters to easily communicate key information. Write a comparison report that recommends a cell phone provider for this company in your state.

4. **Titling**. Evaluate the effectiveness of the following feasibility or comparison report titles. What works well? What changes, if any, would you recommend? Create a more effective title (making up facts if you need to for this exercise).

- Need for an Assistant Production Manager

- Feasibility Report: Exploring Option of Subcontracting Cleaning Services

- Dogday Afternoons: A Decision to Expand Market Presence via a New Marketing Method

- Wiley Financial Web Site Research Report

- Recommendation for Expanded Hours to Increase Revenue at Maloon's Café

CHAPTER 16 QUIZ

Indicate whether the statements 1 through 7 are TRUE or FALSE by writing T or F in the blank.

1. ___ Among the typical questions answered by formal reports are "Why does X happen" and "How do I do X?"

2. ___A formal report may address two or more categories of approaches— comparative, causal, and feasibility.

3. ___A formal report should address only the immediate cause and leave out any distant causes.

4. ___When writing formal reports, you only need to be concerned with the primary audience, not the secondary audience.

5. ___ A letter of transmittal is not part of the report but is submitted on top of a report.

6. ___ The headings and sub-headings in the table of contents EXACTLY match the headings and sub-headings in the report.

7. ___ If your report contains more than 5 terms that your audience might not understand, you should include a glossary of terms in your end matter.

In items 8 through 10, choose the letter of the expression that best completes the statement.

8. ___ A feasibility report (a) excludes evidence that refutes your ultimate recommendation, (b) carefully analyzes both opposing and supporting data, (c) includes opposing evidence but downplays it, (d) b and c, (e) none of these.

9. ___Appropriate content for a letter of transmittal might be (a) acknowledging individuals who helped with the report, (b) referring to specific portions of the report, (c) offering personal observations (d) a and b, (e) a, b, and c.

10. ___A table of contents should include (a) the title page, (b) letter of transmittal, (c) the abstract, (d) tables and figures, (e) c and d.

Additional Fill-In the Blank and Short Answer Questions

11. A list of sources at the end of your report is called _____ in APA style and _____ in MLA style.

12. List at least three different strategies you can use to create an understandable structure for your readers.

CHAPTER 17

Proposals

Proposals encourage an audience to take some form of direct action: to authorize a project, purchase a service or product, or support a specific plan for solving a problem. While a recommendation report answers the question "Here's what we should do and why?" a proposal maps out the steps for getting it done.

The chapter distinguishes between solicited proposals, which are requested by the audience, and unsolicited proposals, which have not been requested. Another distinction is between informal proposals, which may take on the format of emails or memos, and formal proposals, which should be formatted more like formal reports. Both solicited and unsolicited proposals, informal or informal, fall into three categories: planning proposals, research proposals, and sales proposals.

Regardless of the proposal type, writers need to convince decision-makers to say "yes" to what the writer proposes. To accomplish this, the writer needs to apply effective strategies: thorough, documented research; appropriate format; information tailored to the audience's needs; clear, concise, and direct writing; honest and supportable claims; and a request that the reader take action.

After reading this chapter, students will be able to

- Differentiate between solicited and unsolicited proposals

- Differentiate between formal and informal proposals

- Understand the different functions of planning, research, and sales proposals

- Write an informal proposal

- Write a formal proposal

TEACHING TIPS

Virtually all of your students will likely encounter one or more of these types of proposals in their current or future workplace, so this is a great opportunity to link the coursework to their own lives through class discussion. Ask how proposals might apply in their current or future workplace. A proposal, at its core, is a well-supported request for something to happen. We make these types of requests all the time.

Incorporating Proposals Into the Course

As mentioned in the General Teaching Tips section of this manual, you might consider making an early deliverable towards a final assignment that is an analytical report. The proposal might take the form of a research proposal outlining the key research questions and research strategies to answer those questions. By having students define the parameters of the research and writing phases of their analytical report project by creating a research proposal, you can help them develop key project planning skills as well.

Another approach to proposals, as mentioned in the text, is to provide an opportunity for students to write a formal planning proposal as an alternative to an analytical report. Students would describe in detail how a particular problem might be solved via the solution proposed.

Appealing to the Audience

When you introduce the concept of proposals, reiterate that the statement of the problem and the solution need to focus on what the reader cares about. It's easy for students to lose sight of this persuasive element of proposals. The problem or need might seem clear to the writer, but without linking it to a result or issue that the reader cares about, they will get nowhere with a proposal. Run through some examples of stating the problem in different ways for students to understand this point. So, for example, a grant proposal to purchase new drums for a nonprofit arts organization needs to do more than say "the drums will help us reach more people." Who are the people the funder cares about? What are the funder's priorities? A foundation devoted to homeless youth, for example, might be very interested in helping an organization purchase drums to develop outreach programs for children living in shelters to bring fun experimentation, powerful expression, and team building to that environment. This is a much more powerful

130

message than a general "our organization needs drums to reach more people with music."

ADDITIONAL EXERCISES

1. **Evaluating Proposals.** Locate a proposal, either on the Web or through business or organization contacts with which you are familiar. Identify which type of proposal it is (planning, research, or sales) and whether it is solicited or unsolicited. Evaluate the proposal according to the Strategies on page 345 of the text. Also, imagine that you had written the proposal and run through the Checklist for Proposals on page 347. What works well about this proposal? What changes might improve its effectiveness?

2. **Matchmaking.** Nonprofit organizations apply a great amount of time to understanding their potential funders so that they can appropriately craft their proposals. Working in groups of three, seek out a nonprofit organization that has a funding need for a particular project they are interested in implementing. Using foundation resources on the Web, research potential funders for this project by looking at the priorities of the funding agencies.

   Evaluate these potential funders by asking questions such as the following:

   - What types of needs are they interested in addressing? For example, are they specifically interested in serving particular populations?

   - What geographical priorities might they have?

   - What solutions are they interested in funding? For example, some funders do not want to fund capital improvements. Others may not want to fund staffing.

   Based on your research, which three funders should the organization pursue? Why? What, if any, alterations might the organization need to make to its initial project idea to appeal to these funders? Write a memo with this information, addressed to the executive director of the organization you have identified.

3. **Online Grant Proposals.** Increasingly, grantors are requiring online proposals either in addition to or instead of paper proposals. Use the Web to research at least three different foundations that require such proposals.

131

Considering the Strategies for Proposals presented in Chapter 17, what, if any, additional items or changes in strategy might you need to apply in online grant proposals? What challenges might you see in using an online proposal process versus a paper-based proposal process?

4. **Requests for Proposals**. Imagine that you are part of a firm that needs a product or service (decided on what that might be). You have been given a limited budget that must be used in this fiscal quarter. You want to make the best use of these resources, so you have decided to invite bidders to submit proposals for this product. Design and write a request for proposals (RFP) that bidders can respond to so they can persuade you that their product or service will best meet your needs. The RFP should be limited to one page in length.

CHAPTER 17 QUIZ

Indicate whether the statements 1 through 7 are TRUE or FALSE by writing T or F in the blank.

1. ___ Whether solicited or unsolicited, all research proposals are formal.

2. ___ The logical flow of proposals, regardless of type, should move from problem/situation to solution/resolution.

3. ___ Formal proposals have the same format as formal reports.

4. ___ Research proposals can use technical language appropriate for experts in the field.

5. ___ If there are limitations in the solutions you are proposing, be sure to acknowledge them in the proposal.

6. ___ A specific call to action is not necessary in a proposal, because it is implied.

7. ___ Unlike in reports, it is not appropriate to include documentation of sources in your proposal.

In items 8 through 10, choose the letter of the expression that best completes the statement.

8. ___ A proposal for improving your company's morale, requested by the vice president in charge of personnel, probably would be classified as (a) a solicited, internal research proposal, (b) an unsolicited, external planning proposal, (c) a solicited, internal planning proposal, (d) a sales proposal, (e) none of these.

9. ___ The key difference between proposals and reports is that (a) proposals need to accommodate a variety of audiences, (b) proposals answer the question "What should we do?", (c) proposals answer the question "How should we do it?", (d) a and b, (e) b and c.

10. ___ Besides being clear, the proposal plan must be (a) inexpensive, (b) highly optimistic, (c) creative, (d) realistic, (e) a and d.

133

Additional Fill-In the Blank and Short Answer Questions

11. An internal, informal planning proposal might take what two formats?

12. Three types of proposals are _____ , _____ , and _____ .

CHAPTER 18

Digital Communication: Email, Instant Messages, Blogs, Wikis, and RSS Feeds

Chapter 18 begins several chapters of discussion about different types of digital media. From day-to-day interactions among employees to ongoing interactions with clients and customers, digital media pervade virtually every aspect of workplace communication today.

Email. This chapter discusses email as the most common form of workplace communication with the advantages of being able to reach many people very quickly at any hour. However, because of how easily email gets forwarded, the writer has little control over the ultimate audience. Paper forms of communication are preferable if more control is needed. Unlike personal email, which might include a high degree of informality and spelling or grammar errors, workplace email should be well organized, have a professional tone, and use a polished writing style.

Instant Messaging. Another key form of digital communication is instant messaging (IM). This form is most appropriate when immediate, live communications are needed, particularly among people within a company. Although useful for brief, rapid exchanges, IM is not a good medium for the kind of written communication that requires careful planning, composing, and editing. Email is preferable if the writer needs to attach documents to a message or needs a permanent record of the transactions. The chapter provides a number of strategies for optimizing the effectiveness of IM communications.

Blogs. Blogs are interactive online forums. Companies use internal blogs to enhance internal conversations within the company and external blogs to enhance its public conversation with customers. Wikis are a type of blog that allow users to not only comment on earlier postings but to also edit them. Companies use them to facilitate teamwork and collaboration.

<u>RSS Feeds</u>. The final form of digital communication covered is RSS feeds, which allow users to leverage time by using a retrieval program that delivers summaries of blogs or news items to subscribers.

<u>Legal Issues</u>. Because of how easily digital communications are accessed and forwarded, copyright and privacy issue need to be carefully considered.

After reading this chapter, students will be able to

- Identify advantages of using email in the workplace

- Determine if email is the correct form of communication in a given situation

- Compose a well-organized, stylistically appropriate email

- Identify advantages and disadvantages of using IM in the workplace

- Conduct a successful workplace communication using IM

- Explain the workplace functions of internal blogs, external blogs, wikis, and RSS feeds

- Understand basic issues about copyright and privacy in digital communication

TEACHING TIPS

Email Netiquette—Learning Through Past Errors

Though email is the most common form of communication, it is also one of the most misused forms of communication. Sometimes, it is easiest to learn what TO do by learning what NOT to do. Ask your students early on about ways in which they have seen email improperly used. Through this discussion, you can brainstorm netiquette rules that will include and even go beyond the material presented in the text.

Hands-On Experience

The best way for students to learn about the other forms of communication presented in this chapter is by having students use these technologies as part of your other assignments. You might, for example, integrate a wiki tool into one or more group assignments you have in the course. Similarly, you might ask students to create a blog throughout the semester on their own discoveries about technical communication or about a topic of interest to them. If you have students research particular topics, you might invite them to subscribe to RSS feeds from related Web sites that can serve as resources.

Exploring the Legal and Ethical Side of Electronic Communication

Though only a small part of the chapter addresses these issues, it is important to stress the legal and ethical implications of electronic communications. Students often view these as ephemeral communications without realizing their staying power and potentially far-reaching consequences. You might bring in case studies of misuse of email, for example, as well as the key role that email evidence has played in cases involving other legal issues. Similarly, it is important students understand that a public blog does not mean the writers have given up their copyright.

ADDITIONAL EXERCISES

1. **Formatting Email without Style Tools.** Increasingly, people are reading their email on their phones rather than their computers. Often, any style considerations you might include such as bolding, italics, or bullets, disappear when the recipient views your emails in this way. Find an email you have written that applied these types of styles. How might you format the email without these styles so that the reader can still get a sense of the organization? Create a plain text version of your previously styled email.

2. **Evolving Forms of Electronic Communication.** Working in groups of four, explore a form of electronic communication that is not covered in this chapter but has emerged as a growing form of communication for businesses. Two examples are Twitter and social bookmarking, but you might explore a different example as well.

   - What value does this form of communication add to businesses and workplace communication?

- What are examples of how particular businesses have applied this type of communication?

- What are the potential downsides or cautions of this type of communication?

- What are three tips for using this form of communication effectively?

As a team, create a wiki page using a free wiki tool such as PBWiki to report your findings. Share a link to your wiki page with your classmates.

3. **Blogging**. Blog writing has its own unique style that is quite different from email, memos, reports, or other forms of communication. On the Web, research tips for writing for blogs. Drawing from at least five different sources, compile the top 10 tips you would tell someone wanting to start a blog-writing business. After you have your top 10 tips, choose a blog you are interested in following and evaluate how well that blog seems to follow these strategies.

4. **RSS Feeds for Business**. One key use of RSS feeds is to easily add fresh content to an existing Web site. By incorporating RSS feeds into a company's Web site, the company can include new information for readers without having to write all content themselves. You have been hired by a health and wellness company to research and recommend three RSS feeds for its site. Using an RSS feed directory or some other resource to find appropriate sites to draw from, what are three RSS feeds that might add value to customers visiting the health and wellness company's Web site? What is the credibility of the organization creating the feeds? Does the style and tone of these potential feeds seem appropriate? What, if any other issues must the company consider when deciding whether to incorporate your recommended feeds into the Web site? Write an email to the Web-marketing department briefly describing your recommendations and your reasons for them.

CHAPTER 18 QUIZ

Indicate whether the statements 1 through 7 are TRUE or FALSE by writing T or F in the blank.

1. ___ For most simple correspondence, email is the correct format to use.

2. ___Use of bullets, headings, and italics is inappropriate in short communications like email.

3. ___When discussing different topics, you should have different IM threads.

4. ___Blogs can help enhance relationships with customers.

5. ___ Email messages are automatically copyrighted.

6. ___ "RSS" in the phrase "RSS feed" stands for "Retrieval Service System."

7. ___ An RSS "aggressor" is someone who strips data from a Web site in order to prevent others from finding it.

In items 8 through 10, choose the letter of the expression that best completes the statement.

8. ___ When creating workplace emails (a) try to incorporate emoticons for greater connection with your audience, (b) don't worry too much about proper spelling and grammar, since everyone knows how quickly email is written, (c) apply a conversational, informal style, (d) avoid the dangers of netiquette, (e) none of these.

9. ___Use instant messaging (a) when quick exchanges are needed, (b) instead of email because most people prefer it, (c) when you need an electronic record of the transactions, (d) for communications with customers or clients, (e) b and c.

10. ___Internal corporate blogs (a) generally waste employee time, (b) cannot take the place of email, (c) support employee knowledge sharing, (d) are not a replacement for face-to-face meetings, (e) none of these.

139

Additional Fill-In the Blank and Short Answer Questions

11. Describe four potential uses for internal corporate blogs.

12. What is the purpose of an RSS feed?

CHAPTER 19

Online Videos and Podcasts

Yet increasingly, workplace communicators have come to discover the power and potential of using online videos and podcasts as ways to make information easily accessible to wide numbers of customers, clients, students, technical experts, and others.

Today's technical communicators need to think about the "literacy affordances" of different types of media—the features and characteristics that are built into the experience of using different types of technology. Online videos and podcasts, for example, are relatively easy to distribute and produce. More than any other medium, videos integrate the different human communication forms (modalities) such as sound, eye contact, movement, physical gestures, illustrations, and even some text. However, unlike Web sites, videos and podcasts are not interactive and are not easily updated. The choice of medium should arise from the needs of the audience and purpose of the communication.

Both podcasts and videos need to be carefully scripted. In the case of podcasts, it is particularly important that there is not any "dead air" so that every part of the podcast session includes sound. Because podcasts are purely audio, more careful attention to orientation strategies are helpful for the listener. A clear introduction gives listeners a mental map and a preview of the material. The body should include organizing touchstones such as "Now that we have covered X, let's move on to Y." Finally, a conclusion should summarize what was covered and provide contact information (such as a URL) where listeners can find additional information or download other podcasts.

After reading this chapter, students will be able to

- Compare the key differences

- Compare the key differences of different media used for technical communication

- Determine the appropriate audiences for online videos and podcasts

- Identify the advantages of using online videos

- Script and record an effective online instructional video

- Identify the advantages of using podcasts

- Script and record an effective podcast

TEACHING TIPS

While your students will likely all be consumers of podcasts and online videos, they are unlikely to have experience using or creating either of these for business purposes.

Evaluating Quality of Podcasts and Videos

While the chapter focuses primarily on the issues related to creating quality podcasts and videos, this is also a good time to reiterate the importance of being a critical consumer of all information, in whatever form. You might want to refer your students to the criteria for researching you introduced in Chapter 3. Ask students what they need to determine whether the podcasts or videos might be good sources? How might these guidelines inform the type of decisions they make when creating podcasts and videos?

Producing Podcasts and Videos

While scripting a podcast or video can engage learners, actually seeing their scripts come alive as a podcast or video is an experience that really excites them. If possible, try to incorporate production of a podcast or video into your course. This can be a difficult process, though, for some students who are less

142

comfortable with the technology. Therefore, it is helpful to make these types of projects into group assignments. As students assign their roles within the groups, students who are more technology phobic can choose other roles that are less stressful. Regardless of the roles, everyone in the group will experience what it is like to be part of a writing and production team.

ADDITIONAL EXERCISES

1. **Podcasts and Videos In Context.** Many Web sites are integrating podcasts and videos. Find a company or nonprofit organization Web site that uses one or more podcasts or videos.

    - What is the purpose of the communication (instructional, informational, or persuasive)?

    - What is the primary audience for this message?

    - How effective was the choice of medium in the context of this Web site? Would another medium or an additional medium have been more effective? (e.g. a written script of the available podcast AND the podcast itself)

    - Choose one of the videos or podcasts on the site to review—how well was the script and delivery designed and implemented? What changes would you suggest to the Web site owner to make it even more effective?

2. **Creating a Personal Connection via Video.** Nonprofit organizations often use videos to help inspire people to get involved. Choose a nonprofit organization you are interested in and develop a script for a 2-minute video presentation. As you develop the script, use a two-column structure. On the right column, include the text of the audio. On the left column, indicate any visuals that the viewer would see while the audio is taking place. Rarely is a talking head alone visually engaging. Think creatively about what the potential audience might find interesting and compelling to watch. Be sure to test your script to see if it really can fit within the 2-minute timeframe.

3. **Choosing Wisely.** As part of an effort to encourage ongoing learning in a company in your field, the training department has asked employees to nominate top podcasts to include in its monthly podcast recommendations.

143

To ensure that these podcasts are carefully screened, each podcast needs to be nominated by at least three employees to be included.

Find two other students in your course who are interested in your field of study. Together, you will be an employee team that will come up with a recommended podcast. Decide on your team's top pick based on your criteria for a quality podcast. You can nominate a single podcast or a podcast series that includes ongoing or multiple, individual segments. In addition to the structural and production characteristics of the podcasts, be sure to consider basic elements of being a savvy consumer of information. What qualifies as a credible, reliable resource for your colleagues to rely upon? (You might want to refer to Chapter 3, *The Research Process in Technical Communication*).

For your nomination, include the following: names of "employees" sponsoring the podcast, topic, name of podcast and link to the podcast, reasons for nomination.

CHAPTER 19 QUIZ

Indicate whether the statements 1 through 7 are TRUE or FALSE by writing T or F in the blank.

1. ___ Since it is important to use the latest, most cutting-edge technology, you should be sure to incorporate podcasting into your communications.

2. ___ Most online videos are used for instructional purposes.

3. ___ Video multi-modality means that something is distributed in different ways such as online, via DVD, or through TV broadcast.

4. ___ Music should be included throughout an instructional video to be sure the audience stays engaged.

5. ___ Online videos can be used to inform, persuade, or instruct.

6. ___ Like videos, podcasts are multi-modal.

7. ___ There should be some points of silence in a podcast so that the listener can have a break from sound in order to process the information.

In items 8 through 10, choose the letter of the expression that best completes the statement.

8. ___ Examples of literacy affordances include (a) limited distribution, (b) readability in real-time, (c) hyperlinks allowing for easy navigation, (d) a, b, and c, (e) a and d.

9. ___ Scripts include (a) the words that actors will say, (b) direction for the movements of the actors, (c) descriptions of the visuals, (d) images that will be included, (e) all of these.

10. ___ When preparing for a podcast (a) design in time for silence on air so that the listeners can have an aural resting point, (b) avoid practicing, since this will lose the spontaneous feel of a podcast, (c) follow the "introduction-body-conclusion" structure that is familiar and helpful for audiences in other communication situations, (d) avoid confusing listeners with repetitive information such as transcripts, (e) a and d.

145

Additional Fill-In the Blank and Short Answer Questions

11. What are three reasons why you might NOT want to use podcasting?

12. The two literacy affordances that might make a paper-based document more preferable than a podcast are _____ and _____.

CHAPTER 20

Web Pages

This chapter introduces the basics of writing and designing Web pages. Web pages have a number of advantages over print-based documents. They are more easily updated at negligible cost, interactive, and take up minimal space for storage of information.

Both print documents and Web pages must follow the same basic principles of understandable structure and readable style (Chapter 6), audience-centered visuals (Chapter 7), and a user-friendly design (Chapter 8). However, because Web pages and print pages are read differently, some of these elements play out differently in the online environment.

- **Structure:** Rather than outlines, the initial organizing tool for creating Web sites is storyboards or site maps, which visually lay out the relationship between the different pages on the site. When the information on the page is created, it needs to be in short chunks. The sequencing of the information should be logical, but the way in which users may actually use the information may be in a very different order than intended because of the nonlinear nature of the Web sites.

- **Style:** As with print documents, writing for the Web needs to be clear, concise, fluid, and personable. However, because of the small chunking of information on the Web, conciseness is particularly important.

- **Visuals:** Bolding and underlining should not be used for emphasis, because on the Web these styles are usually cues for links. Bulleted and numbered lists are used more generously to chunk information. Finally, running heads and feet and tables of contents are generally not needed for Web sites.

In designing Web sites, communicators need to consider ethical and leader issues. Because of their broad reach, manipulation and distortion on the Web can have far-reaching consequence. Legal issues on the Web include copyright infringement and invasion of privacy.

A final issue addressed in this chapter is the advantages of posting PDF files to Web sites when the format needs to appear exactly as the document was originally designed, appearing the same in print and on the screen. In addition, PDFs are useful on the Web because they can be format-protected in order to avoid alteration or manipulation in any way, allowing greater protection of the copyright. PDFs also allow for posting of longer documents without chunking the information for the Web.

After reading this chapter, students will be able to

- Recognize the advantages of offering information on Web pages rather than in printed form

- Consider audience and purpose before designing and writing a Web page

- Identify the various Web page elements

- Design and write an effective Web page

- Weigh the ethical and legal issues involved in creating Web pages

- Understand in which situations PDF files may be appropriate on a Web page

TEACHING TIPS

Today's Web pages are increasingly dynamic and interactive, integrating the technologies students will learn about in Chapters 18 and 19 as well as other new media technologies that will inevitably have emerged by the time you work with this textbook. Devote some time in class to discussing how the different electronic communication tools serve the audience and purposes of Web sites.

Emphasizing Legal and Ethical Implications

More than any other genre of writing in the course, students will be most familiar with Web sites as a source of information. Yet, the ethical and legal use of Web sites is perhaps the least understood area. Emphasize that free access does not mean open use for all purposes. The idea that they might need to obtain permission to use Web-based content will be a novel concept to many students. They also need to understand that even if they obtain permission, are exempt through fair use, or do not need permission because the material is in the public domain, they still need to properly credit their sources (an ethical issue).

Exploring Pocket-Sized Design

Ask how many of your students regularly visit Web sites via their cell phones, and you'll find that this is, indeed, a popular way to access sites. Explore with your students frustrations they have with viewing sites this way. Ask them about the types of design alterations that might make sites easier to view online. This discussion emphasizes the course-wide theme of thinking of the audience and the context of use when designing documents.

ADDITIONAL EXERCISES

1. **Ethical Use of Web Sites.** As emphasized in the text, it is important to avoid committing plagiarism by properly crediting your sources of information, whether those sources are online or paper-based. Using Appendix A as a resource, develop a proper documentation for three Internet articles you find interesting. Choose MLA, APA, or CSE style for all three of your references. For each source, create a parenthetical reference (the reference that is placed in the text where the source is being used) and documentation that would appear at the end of the document (MLA calls these "works cited," APA and CSE call these "references").

2. **Storyboarding a Site.** Outline a site for a daycare facility. Choose either a dog daycare facility, an adult daycare facility, or a child daycare facility as your topic. Using Figure 20.2 as a model, create a site map that shows the main categories of information you would include and how they relate to each other.

3. **PowerPoint Mockup.** Because PowerPoint includes the ability to create links to different pages from images or text within a page, this is a helpful

tool for creating a rough working version of a Web site without having to use full Web development software for an initial mockup. Representative images, graphics, and text can serve as stand-ins for more robust versions that might be developed later. This is a helpful way to give teams a more visual representation of a site to respond to early in the development phase.

Step 1. Work in teams of three for this exercise. Using the Storyboarding Site Exercise 2 scenario, create a mockup of the site you have outlined. For at least five of the individual pages of the site, create a quick visual layout with headings and text formatted to give the development team a better sense of the type of site you want to create. If you plan to include podcasts, videocasts, or other multimedia elements, create a stand-in representation for it at this point (either as text or a visual image).

Step 2. Once your team has developed its site, walk through your site by presenting it to another team. Describe why you made the decisions you did and any areas for which you would like feedback. Also invite any other feedback they might want to provide.

Step 3. Use the other team's feedback to develop a plan for the next stage in your development. Write up a 1-page revision plan that includes new ideas you gleaned from the feedback you would like to adopt, ideas you decided to set aside, and any further areas of research you might need before deciding on further revisions.

4. **Permissions**. If you would like to use material from a Web site and incorporate it into a document you are working on, it is important to obtain permission, if needed. Find an image on a Web site that you find interesting. Check the Web site's terms of use policy, if there is one, to see if there is any guidance on what, if any, permissions have been granted for using the material on the site.

- From the policy's wording, what uses are explicitly allowed?

- Which uses are specifically banned?

- What further actions might you take to obtain permissions for use of this image in a company Web site?

150

Create a brief report describing the parameters of use for this image and what further actions might be possible for obtaining permission to use the image.

CHAPTER 20 QUIZ

Indicate whether the statements 1 through 7 are TRUE or FALSE by writing T or F in the blank.

1. ___ Logical sequencing is not necessary when designing Web pages because users will rarely follow it.

2. ___ Readers expect more visuals on Web pages than they usually expect in printed documents.

3. ___ If you are only linking from your Web page to another Web page, you do not need to obtain copyright permission.

4. ___ Text set to unjustified right margins is easier to read on a screen than text set to justified right margins.

5. ___ Windows and orphans are irrelevant in Web page design.

6. ___ Online text should be 8–10 point serif font.

7. ___ A storyboard provides a detailed sketch of a Web page.

In items 8 through 10, choose the letter of the expression that best completes the statement.

8. ___ Providing documents online allows for all of the following EXCEPT (a) interactivity, (b) automatic updating, (c) minimal physical space requirements, (d) linearity, (e) cost efficiency.

9. ___ When applying grid patterns to Web sites (a) avoid altering the grid patterns from one page to the next on a Web site, (b) alter the grid patterns from page to page on the site, (c) use only vertical grid patterns, (d) use only horizontal grid patterns, (e) c and d.

10. ___ For emphasizing specific words or phrases on Web sites, you should use strategies such as (a) color, (b) shaded text, (c) underlined text, (d) a and b, (e) a and c.

Additional Fill-In the Blank and Short Answer Questions

11. Two key legal considerations regarding Web pages are _____ and _____.

12. To post longer documents that were originally in print form on the Web without chunking the information for the Web environment, you might consider using _____ format, which anyone can read using a free downloadable reader.

CHAPTER 21

Oral Presentations

This chapter describes key features of and strategies for designing and delivering five main types of presentations:

1. informative presentations, which provide information

2. training presentations, which teach a particular task or tasks

3. persuasive presentations, which convince people to adopt or change their opinions

4. action-plan presentations, which persuade people to take action

5. sales presentations, which both inform people about a product or service and persuade them to purchase it

Regardless of the presentation type, the basic introduction-body-conclusion structure applies in all presentations, just like in other forms of technical communication. The introduction needs to capture the audience's attention, establish the speaker's credibility, and provide a preview of what to expect in the presentation. The body needs to have a logical organization with transitions. Finally, the conclusion needs to restate the big picture and the main points.

The chapter also guides learners on choosing between impromptu, scripted, or extemporaneous presentation styles. In most workplace situations, the extemporaneous style is most appropriate as it provides somewhat of a script for the speaker and allows the speaker to interact with the audience while following along.

Lastly, this chapter provides specific strategies for preparing and delivering oral presentations and discusses issues related to using presentation software.

After reading this chapter, students will be able to

- informative presentations, which provide information

- training presentations, which teach a particular task or tasks

- persuasive presentations, which convince people to adopt or change their opinions

- action-plan presentations, which persuade people to take action

- sales presentations, which both inform people about a product or service and persuade them to purchase it

TEACHING TIPS

Most of your students will have taken one or more speech classes, either at the high school or college level. The majority of their experiences from these classes may have been from memorizing speeches rather than using a more extemporaneous style more common in the workplace. Engage them in a dialogue that distinguishes the two, having them generate the advantages and disadvantages of each for their own current or future workplace environment. Ask them about the context in which they might find themselves presenting orally to others about an idea, product, service, or issue and what they think they would need to do to be prepared to speak to their potential audience.

Speaking Early and Often.

Though the oral presentation chapter is the last in the chapter, the concept of oral presentations should not be last in your instructional design. Throughout the course, your students should be engaging with each other through short, frequent oral communications, either as individuals or as groups during in-class exercises. This will help them become more comfortable with their peers as an audience and will make any final assignment you may have in oral presentations much less intimidating.

Linking Oral Presentations to a Larger Writing Assignment.

Most technical communication courses include an assignment that students build on throughout the course—some sort of final report or proposal that integrates the concepts they have learned. By also including one or more brief oral presentations about this semester-long project, you can help students see more clearly how written and oral presentation differ and how they need to adjust their message and delivery according to the medium as well as the audience.

Whereas many of the final reports or proposals might be written for a more specialized audience, for example, the oral presentations would need to be tailored to an audience of their peers. Remind students to complete an audience and purpose analysis before they design their presentations. What lingo would they need to define? What would make the content interesting and understandable to this audience?

Students can use the feedback and questions they receive on their oral reports to help with their final revisions to their major course assignment. To help students provide specific feedback to each other and encourage active listening, you could include a brief evaluation form that they complete for each of their peers. For this to be realistic in the given timeframe, you might focus on a few key points:

1. Content: How well did the content seem to address your needs as an audience—did anything seem missing or too detailed?

2. Organization: What organizational aspects worked well? What is one organizational aspect that might have been helpful to you as a listener?

3. Style: What were particularly effective aspects of the delivery style? What one style improvement might have made the presentation even more effective?

As part of any major oral presentation assignment, you will likely want to require students to include some sort of visual support to give them experience with this aspect of presentations. Be sure to remind them to have a backup solution if the technology does not work (such as a printed document and having the file in email as well as a thumb drive).

Thinking Broadly About Visuals.

Students need help reaching beyond boring bulleted lists to more engaging use of presentation software or even other types of visual devices. Brainstorm with students about more powerful uses of visuals they have seen in presentations—you'll be amazed at examples they will come up with! In a presentation about schizophrenia, for example, a psychologist presenter once included full-color overheads of paintings by an artistically talented client. They depicted his cat before, at the onset, and during a full-stage schizophrenic episode. These images helped the audience learn in a very powerful way how perception is shifted during such psychotic episodes and expanded their understanding beyond anything words alone could have accomplished.

ADDITIONAL EXERCISES

1. **Capturing Attention and Clarifying the Purpose.** On the Web, find an archive of a city council presentation by a citizen or consulting group to a city council and watch the presentation. Concentrate specifically on the introduction component of the presentation.

    - Which of the five types of presentations is this, or is it a combination of one or more?

    - What style of delivery is being used? Was it appropriate for the audience and purpose of this presentation?

    - How effectively does the speaker use the introduction to spark the city council's interest in the topic? What other strategies might have been effective?

    Write a brief report for your instructor that describes your findings and evaluation of the introduction.

2. **Phone Presentations**. Increasingly, work teams collaborate remotely, with many presentations occurring via phone conferencing and file-sharing technologies. In groups of 3–4, discuss your experiences with this type of presentation.

- From your experiences, or what you imagine as the needs of this type of presentation, how are these types of presentations similar to and different from face-to-face oral presentations?

- What are five key strategies of success that your group would recommend when planning for this type of presentation?

Share your group's views with the rest of the class in 2–3 minute oral presentation by one or more members of your group.

3. **Using Presentation Software Effectively**. Your text provides some guidance on how to effectively design presentation software. Entire courses are available on the topic. With a group of 3–4 classmates, research additional strategies for effectively using presentation software such as PowerPoint. In a 5–7 minute group-delivered presentation, present seven principles you have found. In your presentation, be sure to apply the strategies you found.

4. **Experimenting with Expression**. Try the following exercise in groups of three. Each person should choose one of the following topics to address in a 2-minute presentation to the other members of the group:

- the benefits and dangers of chocolate

- the benefits and dangers of caffeine

- the benefits and dangers of pizza

Spend 5 minutes to quickly outline your presentation. Then, deliver your presentation topic, but with slightly different delivery styles.

Version 1—stick to the same location (don't move very much) and use your vocal intonations and vocal inflections to emphasize key points and draw in your audience

Version 2—allow your body and hands to be the main agent of emphasis at point in your presentation, rather than your vocal inflections

Version 3—concentrate on your facial expression and eye contact as a mode of expression as you share your information

Version 4—use any combination of styles in your presentation

What have you learned about presentation style from this exercise? Be prepared to discuss this with the larger class.

CHAPTER 21 QUIZ

Indicate whether the statements 1 through 7 are TRUE or FALSE by writing T or F in the blank.

1. ___ A memorized delivery style is usually most effective for a formal report.

2. ___ Flip charts are no longer appropriate now that we have more technological solutions such as PowerPoint.

3. ___ You should always include visuals in an oral presentation.

4. ___ Before giving your talk, you should rehearse it at least once.

5. ___ The more colors, images, and sounds the better to keep your audience engaged.

6. ___ If you like to embellish on the material and enjoy engaging with the crowd, use less slides.

7. ___ If you are interrupted by an audience member who has a question, be sure to address that question right away.

In items 8 through 10, choose the letter of the expression that best completes the statement.

8. ___ When using presentation software, on each slide (a) include no more than 7–9 lines per slide (including the heading), (b) include no more than 15–17 lines per slide (including the heading), (c) include no more than 20 words per bulleted item, (d) include no more than 15 words per bulleted item, (e) none of these.

9. ___ When speaking in front of a group and not using a podium, which of the following practices should you employ (a) find one spot in front of the audience and be sure not to stray, (b) feel free to move around a bit, (c) in a conference room setting, stay seated to mirror your audience, (d) avoid approaching the audience during questions since this may intimidate them, (e) gesture widely to maximize the drama.

10. ___ Extemporaneous delivery style (a) avoids the use of notes and instead involves spontaneously thinking on your feet, (b) is the preferred delivery style in the workplace, (c) allows strict control to meet time limits, (d) is most appropriate when communicating with international audiences, (e) is the ideal delivery style for the highly nervous speaker.

Additional Fill-In the Blank and Short Answer Questions

11. What are the three main tasks generally accomplished by introductions in oral presentations?

12. Rather than creating an outline for a presentation, you might use a _____ to account for both the visual components and the spoken content of the presentation?

CHAPTER QUIZ ANSWERS

Chapter 1

1. T

2. F

3. F

4. T

5. T

6. T

7. T

8. F

9. e

10. d

11. Several options possible. Unlike academic papers, technical documents are reader based, task oriented, context sensitive, and design based. It also utilizes many different formats—written, visual, digital, and oral.

12. Several options possible.

Chapter 2

1. F

2. F

3. T

163

4. T

5. T

6. T

7. F

8. F

9. d

10. d

11. claim, interpretation, and call to action

12. Several answers are possible—this is an applied question to students' lives.

Chapter 3

1. F

2. F

3. T

4. T

5. T

6. F

7. F

8. a

9. e

10. c

11. Several answers are possible—this is an applied question to students' lives.

12. Several answers are possible—this is an applied question for students to consider the audience inclinations of survey choice. Mailed surveys might, for example, be most appropriate for populations that do not commonly use the Internet, such as many seniors.

Chapter 4

1. F

2. F

3. T

4. T

5. T

6. F

7. F

8. a

9. e

10. c

11. Several answers are possible—this is an applied question to students' lives.

12. Several answers possible—this is an applied question for students to consider the audience inclinations of survey choice. Mailed surveys might, for example, be most appropriate for populations that do not commonly use the Internet, such as many seniors.

Chapter 5

1. T

2. F

3. T

4. F

5. F

6. T

7. T

8. F

9. e

10. d

11. alphanumeric or decimal

12. Many answers possible – students are to apply the principles to their own experience.

Chapter 6

1. F

2. T

3. F

4. F

5. F

6. T

7. F

8. T

9. e

10. e

11. nominalization

12. Many answers possible for students to make the sentence more concise.

Chapter 7

1. F

2. F

3. F

4. F

5. F

6. F

7. F

8. e

9. d

10. b

11. Line graphs are preferable when it is important to display more data points.

12. Unlike illustrations, which simply show what something looks like, diagrams show how parts of an object fits together or how mechanisms operate.

Chapter 8

1. F

2. T

3. T

4. T

5. F

6. T

7. T

8. e

9. c

10. e

11. A sans-serif font lacks lines that extend horizontally from the main strokes of a letter. Examples include Helvetica and Arial font.

12. Many answers are possible for this question, as students can develop a number of strategies to achieve the purpose described.

Chapter 9

1. F

2. T

3. T

4. T

5. F

6. T

7. d

8. b

9. e

10. b

11. Several answers are possible. Examples include street address, phone number, and other information that puts the student at risk for identity theft; pictures; irrelevant information not related to the jobs sought

12. Several answers are possible. Scannable résumés, unlike paper résumés, need to use very simple fonts. Formatting features often present in paper-based résumés should be avoided in scannable résumés: bolding, italics, underlining, tabs, centering, etc. Instead, résumés intended for scanning should use ALL CAPS for emphasis and have all text flush to the left margin.

Chapter 10

1. F

2. F

3. F

4. T

5. F

6. F

7. T

8. b

9. b

10. a

11. Adjustment letters respond to claim letters.

12. A writer should consider using an indirect approach when conveying bad or unwelcome news or making an arguable claim.

Chapter 11

1. T

2. T

3. T

4. F

5. F

6. F

7. T

8. a

9. e

10. d

11. term, class, and features

12. Students might choose three of the following: negation, operating principle, analysis of parts, visuals, comparison and contrast, required conditions, and examples.

Chapter 12

1. F

2. T

3.   F

4.   F

5.   T

6.   F

7.   T

8.   T

9.   b

10.   d

11.   visuals and a conclusion

12.   functional and chronological

Chapter 13

1. F

2. T

3. F

4. F

5. T

6. F

7. T

8. T

9. e

10. e

11. clear and exact title

12. standard operating procedures, safety procedures, and medical procedures

Chapter 14

1. T

2. T

3. F

4. F

5. F

6. T

7. T

8. F

9. d

10. e

11. closing summary, descriptive abstract, informative abstract, executive summary

12. accuracy, completeness, conciseness, nontechnical style

Chapter 15

1. T

2. F

3. F

4. T

172

5. F

6. T

7. T

8. e

9. d

10. a

11. progress reports, periodic activity reports meeting minutes, trip reports

12. purpose of the meeting and meeting date

Chapter 16

1. F

2. T

3. F

4. F

5. T

6. T

7. T

8. b

9. e

10. e

11. reference, works cited

12. Students should choose from among five potential ones included in the text: outlining, chunking, sequencing, paragraphing, and heading strategies.

Chapter 17

1. F

2. T

3. T

4. T

5. T

6. F

7. F

8. c

9. e

10. d

11. email or memo

12. research, planning, and sales

Chapter 18

1. T

2. F

3. T

4. T

5. T

6. F

7. F

8. e

9. a

10. d

11. Multiple answers are possible—examples from the text include the following: replace some email transactions, employee trainings, meetings, company updates, employee knowledge sharing.

12. An RSS feed retrieves and delivers summaries of blogs or news items to subscribers.

Chapter 19

1. F

2. T

3. F

4. F

5. T

6. F

7. F

8. d

9. e

10. c

11. Multiple answers are possible—examples from the text include the following: the audience is unfamiliar with podcasting technology; the audience might have a slow Internet connection; audience members may be hearing impaired; the purpose of the communication is not conducive to podcasting such as the need to refer back to information or browse through it easily.

12. accessibility and navigability

Chapter 20

1. F

2. T

3. F

4. T

5. T

6. F

7. T

8. d

9. a

10. e

11. copyright infringement and privacy protection

12. PDF

Chapter 21

1. F

2. F

3. T

4. T

5. F

6. T

7. F

8. a

9. b

10. b

11. capture the audience's attention, establish your credibility, and preview the content

12. storyboard